Thank you Jenny for the years that you have shared and directed me on this amazing journey. Your horsemanship, compassion and friendship is the reason that my life with horses exceeded any dream that I could have imagined on my own!

Thank you Nathan Granner for your powerful uplifting presence in my life. I don't know how you turned out to be this amazing, but there are a world of humans so glad you did. Thank you for sharing yourself and your talent with your proud mother.

Pony Genes

Before I can begin my story, the story starts with my mother. Many girl babies are born with an invisible gene. It is called "love of horses". Little girls, medium size girls and big girls are crazy about horses. Many girl babies and a few boy babies are born this way. They can't help it.

Mom had the mystical horse gene. She was born in 1918 on a farm in southern Iowa. The farm grew hay, beans and corn. Horses were the horsepower for farming. When Mom grew big enough, she wanted a pony more than anything. Her folks said, "Marie, you have to earn the money for that pony. You can pull weeds in the bean fields." Her parents paid her by the weed. She was alive with the dream that she would have her own pony. I do not know the enormous amount a pony went for back then. Mom did tell me the price she got for each weed, but I don't remember. Mom pulled weeds and earned the pony money. She never forgot how hard that was. I've never forgot her stories about it either.

That's when Dan came into her life. He was a bay and white spotted pony. She loved him. Mom and her best friend, Betty, rode their ponies without saddles, without shoes in the summer and in dresses. Man! Betty owned Dimples, and Dimples would do anything for Betty. They rode to the country school. When school was over, they rode their ponies home. Dimples and Dan were a matching set! Did the two sets of parents planned for their daughter-best-friends to have matching ponies?

Betty & Dimples   Marie & Dan

Mom was a year older than Betty. They were the only two younger kids around their rural school. Mom asked if Betty could start school a year early, so Mom wouldn't be the only little kid in the school. The answer was yes. The teacher was Mrs. Johnson. She became my fifth grade teacher. She told me that she remembered teaching my Mom. Mrs. Johnson must have been quite young when she started teaching in the country school to have made it to be my fifth grade teacher. My mother was twenty-five when I was born right at the end of WWII.

Mom and Betty spent tons of time riding their ponies everywhere. Then something happened to my mother's brain that she regretted for the rest of her life…all the rest of her life. She saw kids riding bicycles in town. She decided that she had to have a bike. Money was tight in the late 20's on the farm.

She sold Dan to get the money to buy the bike! This was impractical because she lived on a dirt road. Biking is not fun on dirt or gravel roads! She told me years and years later that she didn't know that she could change her mind and not sell Dan. She wanted to change her mind, but she had made a commitment. She sold DAN! That is the beginning and end of my mother's young pony years. What she didn't know is that the invisible pony gene was going to show up again in her young daughter!

I was four years old when the fifties started. We lived in the same small town in southern Iowa. Osceola had 3500 people and everyone knew everyone! My father served during WWII and was stationed in California. That is why I was born in San Francisco! I had thick red hair and WWII had just ended. No one suspected a redhead baby would emerge from my brown haired mother and father! Yes, red-haired people are a mutant race. I was carried all over the hospital by the nurses and showed off to the patients. When my parents came back to Iowa, my father got job, bought a house and a few years later, built a tiny grocery store beside our house. We went out the front door on the porch and walked into the back door of the store. Later when the store was expanded, I could climb out the side living room window into the storage area of the store. That was cool! It was the hot convenience store of the 50's.

Back then grocery stores stayed open until around 8:00pm. Our stored stayed open until ten o'clock at night. You could run into the store and get something you had forgotten to buy at the big store. We had lots of candy and sliced lunch meat. Later we added soft ice cream and hot dogs. The store was on highway 69. Highway 69 was a highly traveled north and south national route before I-35 was invented. The official store name was North Side Grocery. The town people called it by the real name, "The Little Store". Years later, my father enraged the entire town and painted the store pink. After people stopped being mad about the pink color, the store became known as "The Little Pink Store". You couldn't get directions to go anywhere in town without the Pink Store included in the route directions!

My mother delighted in taking me to the auction barn, just a little farther down the street from Dr. Paul's stable. We would go and watch the horse auctions; because my mother's invisible horse gene had not gone completely dormant. We went a lot and I grew very familiar with the sale barn atmosphere. It was a great place to play. I could run around in the back and look at the horses, go in the small auction-cafe or sit with my mother and watch the auction. It was exciting to watch the horses come in. I can do a great auctioneer imitation at parties!

One day at the auction, I was sitting beside my mother. A horse came in. My mother gasped and said, "THAT's DAN!" That's my pony! We sat there, and she muttered about who was bidding on Dan. Then she raised her hand and we ended up buying Dan! I have no idea how old I was, but this is a very vivid memory. I didn't remember what color Dan was. I remember him as being very big. My mother grew up, graduated from high school, lived through WWII and found the horse of her childhood in an auction barn! The next thing I knew, we had a big horse staked out in our back yard. Let's try to figure out how old he was. Let's guess my mom was eight years old when she got Dan. That would be 1926. He would have been old enough to ride. I was three years old in 1949. So I bet Dan was in his mid 20's.

The neighbor kids came. Three of us rode him at the same time. Dan probably didn't move, but I remember being on him with my friends. Some days later, Dan was transported to my Uncle

Lloyd's farm. He lived out his remaining days in peace. I was shocked when I found pictures of Dan and my mom. I remember him being a tall red horse. Instead he was a bay and white spotted large pony.

When I became an adult, I asked mom, "Who was bidding on Dan at the auction?" She replied, "It was the owner of a pony ride. Dan would have been tied to a "pony ride wheel" the rest of his old life out in the hot sun of the summer."

This is one of my favorite stories about my mother. She bought her pony back. She had a millisecond to decide to buy him. You know how fast those auctioneers go. There was one bidder. She did not have much time to consider things like where she would keep Dan. She had no place to keep him. She did not have time to run home, use the rotary dial phone to call her brother to ask if he would take Dan. She knew Lloyd would take Dan in a minute. She brought him home. We led him home down the sidewalk alongside highway 69. When Mom bought Dan at the auction, her pony genes were reactivated!

Never Lie to a Little Girl with Pony Genes

Across the street in the next block was a stable. My mom would take me over to Dr. Paul's stable to visit the horses. My very first vivid memory of Dr. Paul's stable is that of a newborn palomino foal. We were watching the foal play in a small corral. Dr. Paul's trainer came and haltered the foal. I asked, "Can I ride it?" He told me that the foal was too little for me to ride right now, but I could ride it later. I never forgot that statement. That man lied to me. He never let me ride that horse. I have never forgiven him, either .Never! His sister was in my class at school. Every now and then I told her about how her older brother had lied to me about riding that horse. Never lie to a young girl about riding a horse. The young girl will beat you up when she gets old enough. Girls with pony genes never forget and they are dangerous.

I found this article about Dr. Paul in an online 1948 Rotarian Newsletter:

Dr. Everett W. Paul, is a dental surgeon holding membership in the Rotary club of Osceola. (all those years with Dr. Paul. I never knew he had a first name!) *Horses have been his hobby for 50 years – ever since the day he was given a motherless colt to care for as a 10-year-old farm lad.* {this means that Dr. Paul was probably 60+years old in 1948! I was around 11 years old when Dr. Paul took over my horse education.} *"I raised that colt on a bottle, nursing her along and training her," he recalls. "She grew into a fine five-gaited mare and I rode her until I was ready to start high school." He then sold her to help defray his schooling expenses.*

The love of horse flesh which that colt developed in Dr. Paul has never ceased to grow. Today he has approximately 50 horses, including 25 registered saddle mares, six registered Palomino stallions, and a number of colts. He operates a Palomino farm {I never ever knew that until I found this article!} *outside of Osceola and a stable in town.*

The doctor is perhaps proudest of Paul's Palomino Peavine, a 5-year old stallion which has been publicized in the horsey magazines as "the most golden Palomino in the country." Last year the horse was shown in competition about 35 times, and it came home with "an oat bagfull" of ribbons, including the grand championship of the Council Bluffs Frontier Days show and the Waterloo National Stallion show.

"Palominos," Dr Paul explains, "are a color of horse, not a breed. The color is produced in colts by breeding a Palomino with another breed. "And," he adds, "if you breed Palomino with Palominos, the color may fade away almost to a white"

Horses are a mutual hobby for the Pauls. The doctor's wife, who is also his dental assistant, has a love for the animals which is as pronounced as that of her husband's. In fact, she has brought home more blue ribbons riding the Paul horses than her husband has.

A fancy saddle made especially for Paul's Palomino Peavine has a place of honor in the Paul's den when "off duty". It looks very much in place amid as assortment of trophies, ribbons, and awards.

But don't ask Dr. Paul what it cost. That, he says, he has never told his wife. He will admit, though, that the bridle cost him $650. {note: this was in the year 1948!}

Dr. Paul never had a first name during my childhood. This treasure article that the internet found for me is the first I ever knew his first name. Dr.Paul played a significant role in my childhood horse life. I will never forget him. He crossed my path significantly again not too far down the road of my childhood and teen-age life with horses. I don't think that Dr. Paul would have ever told me I could ride the foal. He was a plain speaking man!

Just so you know, never lie to a little girl child about letting her ride a horse. She will never forget.

Mommy, Daddy, grandpa – Can I have a pony

I grew up watching Roy Rogers, Dale Evans, Trigger, Buttermilk and Bullet on the black and white television (TV). You turned the TV on and let it warm up. If there were no programs on TV, you got to watch a test pattern. There were three TV stations and a big antenna on the top of our house. TV was on in the morning to ten at night. From nine to ten at night, we watched the news.

I watched Hopalong Cassidy and his great white horse, Topper. Hopalong wore a white hat and a black outfit. I grew up watching The Lone Ranger and his white horse, Silver. His companion was Tonto and his paint horse, Scout. Every kid yelled the words, "HI HO SILVER!" as we played our cowboy and Indian games outside. When the bad guys were doing something evil, The Long Ranger always found out. He yelled, "HI HO Silver" as Silver reared up and galloped away to stop the evil cowboys. Oh what a sight that was. A handsome masked man on a beautiful white stallion rearing up and taking off at a gallop. "Hi Ho Silver" are the ringing words of justice about to be served!

I loved Wild Bill Hitchcock the most. The program started with Wild Bill on that little TV screen shooting right at me. He was galloping and shooting at bandits. The bandits were ahead of him. I thought he was shooting right at me. I always hid behind the chair when his program started. I did not want to accidentally be shot. TV was in its infancy then and was magic.

Somewhere along the way, the idea occurred to me that I should have a pony. All little girls with the hidden "pony gene" have this same thought.

We go to our Mommy and ask if "Can I have a pony?" Since you can't delete the pony gene, I imagine my mother was secretly thrilled with the idea that another pony could come into her life.

She told me to go ask my Daddy. We lived in town. We had nowhere to keep a pony. Why that little factoid didn't bother anyone back then still puzzles me. This was a rural small town in Iowa with a lot of fenced pastures and no zoning laws. "What are zoning laws?" those small town people from the fifties would ask.

I went to my Daddy. I remember asking him. "Daddy, can I have a pony?" He acted very sad and told me that he could not afford to buy a pony. He cleverly told me to ask my grandfather. The next time we went to Winterset to visit my grandpa, I did.

Grandpa Charles Kimmel was a WWI veteran. He and my grandmother divorced and he was not able to raise his son. Money would have been tight when he had to pay for her housing and his son's support. He rarely got to give his son "extra" things. My father learned how to make something out of nothing and that's how he made do early in the world.

I was all set. I was the only child and the only grandchild. I had curly red hair and freckles. I was totally cute and I knew it. I was a young actress knowing the subtle ways of being adorable when wanting something. I got my grandfather alone in his shop. I became adorable. I gazed into his eyes, tilted my head just a little and put the desire tone in my voice. It was just him and me.

"Grandpa, would you buy me a pony?" My grandfather must have had horses early in his life. He must have been raised up on a farm. Back in his day, horses were probably $25 and an expensive horse might have been $50. I told him that my father had told me to ask him. He smiled and said, "Yes! I'll buy you a pony."

My memory fades. Here's what I can guess! My face lit up with a huge smile. I screamed I jumped up and down and clapped my hands. Just a guess, mind you. I thanked my grandfather and ran screaming in to tell my mother and father.

Here's another guess. My father must have been stunned and my mother must have started planning the pony search right on the spot!

One day my mother told me she had found me a pony! She had found the pony and called my grandfather to ask if he would spend $200 on a pony in foal, with matching hand carved pony saddle and bridle. Mom told me that my grandfather, Charles Kimmel, was shocked at the price but he said YES! Two hundred dollars was a ton of money back in the 50's! Remember, I was his only grandchild.

A local highway patrol man had bought his daughter a pony. The little girl was terrified of the pony. It wasn't a good match. The pony ruled over the little girl and scared her. That little girl lost her pony gene dream. The Shetland pony, Cricket, became my pony dream instead.

My father never suspected that pony genes would turn his life into pony-hell. Pony hell became fencing the back yard, building a small barn, building a large barn, fencing a city block pony pasture, and spending many winters feeding and watering ponies in frigid frozen Iowa. He loved my mother too much to want her to spend twice a day feeding and watering the ponies in those Iowa winters.

Once again, my mother brought home a pony. We had no fenced lot. We had exactly the same set up as we had when my mother brought home Dan. We had a stand-alone old garage. It was old then. We tethered the pony out in the yard and must have blocked off the garage door to keep the pony in at night. My Dad found out the first meaning of pony hell when he built the pony pasture. We used to have a large back yard and it became a pony pasture. Later he built a tiny perfect pony barn. Nothing was too good for my pony.

Her name was Cricket. When we talked about her, she became Sally Cricket. She was a black pony with a black and white tail.

She was a dominant pony. I remember when I first got her, I was walking in front of her pretending to lead her. (My mother was actually leading her.) Cricket bit my rear because I was too slow. She was a pony boss!

I would guess that I only rode her when my mom was leading her. I was very young. My mother told me that I could not use the saddle until I learned to ride. I had to ride her bareback. Folks back in those days understood horseback riding.

When my father built the pony pasture in the back yard, he made an enemy for life between him and the next door neighbor, Mr. Scott. Mr. Scott was upset that his beautiful backyard was going to be next to a place where manure was to be found. No one in the 50's picked manure up out of the pasture.

Mr. Scott had planted a row of beautiful trees on the edge of his property. They were growing nicely when the pony pasture was being planned. My father researched our property and discovered that the beautiful trees were on our property. He built the fence and Mr. Scott's trees were inside our pony pasture! Mr. Scott ended up with no beautiful trees on his property. There was yelling involved. Yelling between Mr. Scott and my father! Yell at my father and he loses his temper and yells back. The property people were called to give an official opinion. The trees and fence were on our property. We gained four trees, a little bit of contested land and a bitter enemy. Mr. and Mrs. Scott were always nice to me. But, I was terrified of Mr. Scott. That fear and distrust never ended. Yelling is scary for kids.

I think the fence, the Mr. Scott episode and increasing number of ponies forced my mother to find rental pastures.

Who's the Boss?

Cricket was living in a rental pasture the first time I rode her without my mother leading her. My mother decided it was time for me to ride Cricket by myself. I climbed on and told Cricket to go! I remember she did go a few steps and then she laid down! My mother yelled at me to jump off! I jumped off. Thank goodness for the bareback rule. It's way easy to do an emergency dismount without a saddle in your way. We waited till Cricket got back up. My mother told me to get on and ride Cricket at a canter around the pasture to show her that the laying down had been a very bad idea. I remember my mother telling me to go fast. I got Cricket going as fast as I could. I remember it as cantering! I wasn't to let her stop, either. We rode long enough for Cricket to get the true meaning that I had become the boss. Boss little girl takes over the leadership role from the dominant boss pony! It worked! I don't remember any problem with Cricket after that.

Only a mommy that had a pony in her childhood would have known what to do. That was a critical step in my development. If my mother had not known what to do, Cricket would have ended up dominant over me, hurt me in some way and could have been for sale again to another little girl who dreamed of having a pony! WHEW!

LITTLE GIRL'S BEST FRIEND

My mom was talking to the owner of the rental pasture. He pointed at my cute little Cocker Spaniel, Timmy, and said, "That dog has been killing my chickens!" My mother indignantly responded, "Timmy wouldn't kill chickens!" Right then and there, one of the owner's chickens ran out into the yard. Timmy sprang forward, made contact with the chicken and killed it. Yes, the adorable cocker spaniel killed a chicken right in front of my mother and the rental pasture owner. My adorable cocker spaniel, Timmy, was correctly identified as a chicken killer. Can you imagine how humiliated and horrible that experience was for my kind-hearted mother!

My mother forked over money to pay for the alleged number of dead chickens and took Timmy home. Timmy ended up living in a home with people that had nothing to do with chickens. I was on the lookout for another dog. I learned at an early age not to ask my parents if I could have a dog. You just bring the puppy home. It works every time.

Our house and store was across the street from the high school. The janitor of the high school was Felix. He was a great fun person and came over to my parent's store all the time. He loved to pull jokes on my father. One day Felix called me over to the high school. He took me to the broiler room and showed me two puppies that were dumped at the high school. He told me to take the puppies home. I did! What cute puppies. I was thrilled to take both of them. I could not believe my good fortune and Felix's kindness in picking me to take home the puppies.

My father didn't think Felix was the greatest person in the world when he discovered who was responsible for me having two puppies. When he came home from work, I was in the backyard playing with my puppies. I could tell my father was a little upset when he tersely asked me where the puppies had come from. I said, "Felix gave them to me." "WHAT!", his voice accelerated up. I explained about the puppies. My father marched over to the high school. I can't imagine the conversation that he and Felix must have had! My father could not take puppies away from his cute red haired daughter. He was stuck. My cousin, Mary, got one of the new puppies and she was another happy little girl! My cousin lived up the street from me and we had many happy years playing with our sister doggies.

My puppy's name was Snoopy and she lived a long good life. She was a solid black dog with floppy ears and a plume tail. She was my constant companion in everything. Snoopy went with to the pasture and later with me on almost every ride. She and I were a team. We went everywhere. Somewhere in her mid-years, we went on a road riding trip and she started lagging behind on the way home. I remember getting her into the saddle and carried her home. Soon after that, I got Sham ready to leave the pasture. Snoopy didn't come with me. Instead, she walked home, about 3 blocks away. She had to give up following me everywhere. Snoopy lived a long number of years after that as my personal companion. She died after I graduated from college.

My father plotted for the rest of his life how to repay Felix. One trip to the west we discovered burros running free in Nevada. My father was full of plans to capture a burro, ship it home and deliver it to Felix. That would have paid that Felix back for getting me to bring home two puppies!

THE PONY YEARS

This is the 50's! Shetland pony prices go ballistic! Ponies were the hot new thing for all the baby boomer children that were turning five and six. Everyone wanted their kid to have a pony. It was an American dream. Men with incomes discovered Shetland Ponies and started to show them. Our hometown Chevy dealer got into Shetlands and started showing them. His most famous pony's name was Kewpie Doll. She was a gray and white pony. Spotted ponies became big. Sorrel ponies became big. We subscribe to the Shetland Journal magazine. We visit Shetland pony breeders on vacation. My mother is after more pony mares to have more pony babies to sell! She and I started going to Perry, Oklahoma, every summer to the world's largest pony sale. It was a mammoth place. It lasted a week. There was a carnival, food vendors and acres and acres of ponies for sale. I had free run of the entire Shetland pens, auction arena, carnival and food vendors for the week!

I saw a registered Shetland pony stallion sell for $56,000 in the 50's! I watched and listened to the bidding! The auction hammer slammed and the sing-song voice announced, "Sold for $56,000!" That must be like a million dollars in today's world!

We did buy one pony one of the years that we went there. We bought a little pony named Honey. She matched Cricket's first foal…black and white. We entered Honey and Princess in many a 4th of July parade!

Anything pony was a big deal in America. Driving ponies became popular. Adults who fell in love with ponies needed to do something other than take them on walks. They needed to drive their ponies! My father came across a buggy deal too good to pass up. The buggy was too big for a Shetland. My father took off the axle and big wheels and built an axle that would fit bicycle wheels. He cut the shafts down to pony size. My parents bought a harness and I can still remember them marveling and wondering about all the parts. I was allowed to drive Cricket all by myself…with my mother just strolling along beside us. I stupidly sold that harness in the '80s. What could I have been thinking? I want that harness back! I want the buggy. I want my Cricket reincarnated and back. I want my pony gene memories back! I want to relive my happy childhood.

In two years, my mother became a Shetland pony businesswoman. She bought brood mares and a sorrel stallion. At that time, most everyone had gray ponies. Sorrels were rare and sought after. We started producing ponies (some sorrel and some grey) at a rapid rate. I got to train all of them (to lead).

We bought our own pasture by this time. It was about a city block. My parents kept that pasture until all the ponies passed away. They sold the land for way more money than they could have imagined when they bought the city block for $700. I can drive by my former pasture, look at the homes and know my ponies' bones are somewhere in those yards!

The Little Store raffled off a pony colt every year for many years. Customers filled out a coupon when they came in. It was understood that you had to buy something to get a coupon, but that was not really true. One year my mother bought a large pony for the raffle. I got to ride that large pony. He was a blue roan. I called him Sky Blue. One of my best friends in my class won him. Stan and I grew up together and we started kindergarten together. He moved to an acreage just outside the city limits. Stan's sister worked for in The Little Store. I would go to his house and visit both he and Sky Blue. Years later, we wonder if the sister had cleverly manipulated the drawing so her brother could win.

For several years, I got to be in charge of a pony-go-round…free rides for children of customers. It was like a modern day walker. You hitched up the ponies to the arms, put the kids on and they walked around in circles. We had the walker in our pony pasture behind our house. I didn't have much business. The walker took up too much space and did not increase business at the Little Store. It was sold.

The ponies paid for most of my way through college. In the '60's, the bottom fell out of the pony market. No one wanted ponies and those that still did were reluctant to pay the high price for a pony. We had to give away our baby colts. We sold our fillies for ridiculous prices. The pony ride was over!

Dr. Paul's Drill Team

Dr. Paul decided he wanted to be the drill team leader of a fabulous drill team. The drill team consisted of young pony crazy girls. Dr. Paul took us on.

At the time, I was riding a pony for a famous dressage trainer, Austin Smith. His clients brought horses from all over the USA to Osceola, Iowa, to be trained in dressage. One of his clients brought a black and white pony for Austin to train for his little girl. Austin trained that pony up to the point where he needed an experienced pony rider. Trigger became my pony to ride. Black and white Trigger and I matched another pony in the group. Trigger was the smallest pony in the drill team and our position was cemented at the end of the lineup. You can see Trigger and me on the end. I did end up galloping Trigger everywhere, just like Roy Rogers! There is Snoopy in the middle with Dr. Paul. She became the mascot of the drill team as she was always in attendance. Dr. Paul appeared old then.

The Osceola Saddle Club decided that they would ride from Osceola to Des Moines in August to attend the Iowa State Fair. The mileage on the highway from Osceola to Des Moines was right around 50 miles. We had to ride further than that as we had to take the back roads, not the main highway that led straight to Des Moines. We had to make it to the designated campsites at night. It took us three days to ride that far. I rode Trigger the first year. By the time the real owner of Trigger got her pony, he was a wonderful child's pony. He had been there and done that with me! I had no clue about dressage, but Trigger's owner got a great pony!

Every small town in southern Iowa and northern Missouri had a saddle club. Each saddle club held a horse show during summer. One of the classes was "drill team". Dr. Paul's drill team was the only girls' team. All the other drill teams were adults.

The girls' drill team was fabulous. Dr. Paul made us riders. We practiced. We were all fearless girls. At the horse show, our drill team rode into the arena at single file at a gallop. We cantered and galloped through our patterns. Visualize ten cute girls on ponies galloping in formations of two, four and then all ten of us side by side. We split up into lines of five ponies meeting and weaving in and out. We did a large figure eight and a pony from each direction had to alternate crossing in the middle of the figure eight. Remember, this was done at a canter or a gallop. The faster you go, the harder it is to control the exact speed needed to make your split. The highlight pattern was our wagon wheel. The pony in the inside of the wheel had to turn a circle in place. . The ponies on the outside had to gallop the circle really fast to stay even. Noses and tails remained side by side, but the outside ponies were galloping and the inside pony was turning in place. At the end we would line up in a row in front of the judge. Sherry Scholl would ride her black and white pony to the front and ask him to rear. Then we galloped out of the arena. We always won first place. I'm the black and white pony on the end. The adult drill teams trotted their patterns. Cantering was just a little too much for them. The adult drill team was very dull compared to us cute little girls with our ponies. Our saddle club adults tried to vote Dr. Paul out of the saddle club so he could not train us. Their motivation was to eliminate our drill team so they could win! They were horrified to find out that Dr. Paul was not a member of the saddle club. They could not vote him out! It did not matter that he was not a member of the saddle club! There was no way to stop him from being our drill team leader! Those jealous adults just wanted to beat us in the show arena! Their horse genes were jealous!

WHAT IS DRESSAGE

One day my father and I went to Austin's barn to ask him a question. Austin was in the midst of training one of the high level dressage horses. You realize at the time, dressage to me was "what Austin Smith did with horses". My world was Shetland ponies, quarter horses, American Saddlebred horses, saddle club and society horse shows.

My father and I went into the arena where Austin proceeded to do leg yield canter, extended trot, lead changes every other step, the trot in place (piaffe) maneuver and other awesome things. My father and I watched in awe. I tried to figure out how he was telling that horse to do all those things. Occasionally his crop would be held in a different position, but that did not seem to be the secret. There seemed to be no different body movements from Austin. When Austin stopped his horse, I asked Austin, "How do you get the horse to do all that?" Austin probably debated within himself with the answer. Probably he figured out that I would not have a chance of understanding the answer. Only after I became a Level 3 student in the Parelli study of natural horsemanship would I have understood his answer. Austin answered, "Oh, it's a little bit of this and a little bit of that." I had no more questions.

Later in my adulthood before we moved to the farm, I decided to take horseback riding lessons. I found a place in the city. I called and got signed up for a lesson. The person on the phone said I would be taking dressage lessons. Dressage Lessons! I would be learning how to do flying lead changes, piaffe, and canter sideways? It seemed a little advanced for me not having ridden a horse in 30 years! I took the lesson. Dressage was explained to at my lesson as walking and trotting a horse. I was required to post. I knew how to post 30 years ago, but my body struggled to keep in rhythm with this great big Saddlebred horse. This horse had quite a bit more animated trot than my Dixie Lee Stonewall! It was humiliating. I concluded that I was too fat to post. I never scheduled another dressage lesson.

The Parelli training teaches students from the very beginning of knowledge about a horse up to higher levels of training. They did not used dressage terms in Level 3, but that's what I ended up doing, dressage. I would have understood Austin's answer 40 years later.

Sham

It was time for me to graduate from Shetland to large pony. My mother went out into the world and a buckskin large pony showed up in our backyard lot. His name when he came was Davy Crocket. He was an unstarted two-year-old. My mother was worried about me riding an unstarted horse. Of course, I wasn't worried, being full of 11 year old confidence. Mother led Sham around while I rode. After a while, she let me go at it alone and we never looked back.

I wanted to rename the large pony. I had just read King of the Wind and learned that Sham in Arabic meant SUN. That became his barn name. Sham looked just like Dale Evan's horse, Buttermilk. Thus Sham, Davy Crocket, Buttermilk JR became his name...but I called him Sham. I had to explain his name to everyone for the rest of his life and still today!

I put a bridle on him and crossed the reins so he would learn to neck rein.

Sham had just finished a brutal winter in the country. He was a young horse and with the snowstorms, he didn't get enough to eat. Being it was the 50's, my mother couldn't get out to him much during the horrid winter. She had no place to contain Sham to feed him. He was running with a herd of horses…older horses that drove Sham away from the food.

When we got Sham back in the spring, he was a bunch of ribs. We started feeding quarts of oats 3-4 times a day. Trigger had gone to his real little girl owner. Bony Sham and I were welcomed into the drill team. Thank goodness, Dr. Paul allowed us to join, even though we made the drill team look bad. Since my place was at the back of the line, Dr. Paul placed us in the back, even though Sham was taller than about half of the ponies. There we were, a tall scarecrow, making the whole drill team out of balance. Never a word did I hear a complaint from Dr. Paul, other parents or my drill team partners.

Sham gained his weight back and we were granted a place in the drill team to match his height.

Sham and I were the best of friends. He was a barrel racer, a pole bender and a large pony pleasure class competitor. I rode him to the fairgrounds to practice in the arena. I rode out in the country with my riding partner, Sherry Scholl. On summer days, we took horse cruises out of town. Occasionally we would stop and steal apples and cherries in people's yards. Only once were we caught. We would head down a gravel road and ride for 5-6 miles. If Sherry didn't go, I went alone. I dealt with cars out on gravel roads. I thought nothing of that then. Now I think, "What could my mother have been thinking to let me ride out on gravel roads!" We didn't have parks and trails to ride. We didn't have trailers to take our horse to the park. After all, I couldn't even drive yet. I had to ride everywhere. In junior high I had a boyfriend. He lived in the country about five miles out of town on Highway 69. An abandoned train track ran along Highway 69. Sham and I walked, trotted and cantered on that abandoned track to visit my boyfriend! I pretended that I was visiting his sister, but I flirted with my boyfriend as much as I could. Then I got back on Sham and rode home.

The Osceola Saddle Club rode again to the Iowa State Fair. I rode Sham this year. On our first overnight stop, Sham acted like something was hurting him. He pointed at his stomach. He laid down and stood up. My mother and I had no idea what was wrong. Another rider told us Sham had colic and he might not make it. There were no cell phones. There was no calling the vet. We just prayed he would make it, and he did!

At this time of my life, my parents had a pickup. My father built a box on the bed. It had no windows, just a door where we could get in and out. We slept on Army cots in that airless enclosure. That is where my mother and I stayed during our overnight camp outs. I would like to add that the Iowa State Fair occurs in August. How hot could it have been camping in an airless space during the August nights? Good Gad!

Mr. Willis Todden, my trainer, taught me how to do all the racing and showing events. Mr. Todden worked with Sham and me to sidepass, get both canter leads and maintain our gait. Sham ran poles and barrels and did the lead changes. I lived on Sham. If the pony class judge was a quarter-horse-loving judge, we usually won the class. If the judge was a Saddlebred-loving judge, we usually placed.

Saddle club rules said kids couldn't show in pony events at the age of 15. Sham's show career terminated at that time. When I started riding my new horse out of the pasture and away, Sham stopped drinking water. I had to ride my new horse and then ride Sham. He started drinking his water again. He hated not getting to go with me out into the world.

DIXIE LEE STONEWALL

It was time to get me a horse. When I was in my fifties, my mother told me that she had not wanted me to own a quarter horse because she was afraid that I would get hurt barrel racing. Instead, we purchased a crazy American Saddlebred.

Dixie Lee Stonewall was the most beautiful horse I had ever seen. Her Saddlebred head was gorgeous. We went somewhere in mid Iowa to see her. The owner rode her and then I did. It went perfectly and we bought her. Imagine my mother's surprise when the nice horse at the seller's house (probably drugged or rode 100 miles that day) turned into a frantically scared horse at our house! Dixie tried to jump out of the truck on her way to her new home. That was before we had horse trailers.

Horses rode in trucks with high sideboards. She was insane on the truck ride to our house. They got her in the truck and tied her short. She was scared to death and tried to commit horse suicide. Thank goodness, I didn't see that. After she rested for a day at her new home, I went out to the barn to bridle and saddle her. She was nuts when I tried to get a bridle on her. She stuck her head 1,000 miles up into the air.

Dixie had to be sent to Mr. Todden. I couldn't get the bridle on her. Dixie Lee Stonewall was beyond my skill level.

Mr. Todden was one of the original natural horse trainers. He trained mules for WW I in California. I was told that many a horseman wanted to keep Mr. Todden in California to help train their horses, but he came back to Iowa. I have no memory of what his real occupation was.

Dixie came back from Mr. Todden, a manageable horse with a few hang-ups with which I could deal with the help of weekly training lessons. Our first six months were quite a struggle. Dixie had a morbid hatred for spurs. The first time I touched her with a spur (under the direction of Mr. Todden) her mouth snaked around, and she tried to eat my boot. It took a while for me to get my boot out of her mouth. There are many reasons to wear boots when riding a horse!

She also had a huge fear of sticks…like a riding crop. What her owner had done to her with spurs and the crop made a deep impression on her. She got so that she could tolerate the crop but always shuddered when I tapped her rear with the crop.

When I first started riding Dixie on the roads around town, she was scared of anything that moved. She was a sideways jumper. She spooked straight up and straight sideways at the same time. I managed to stay with her as she became used to the world. If that would happen to me now at my tense age, I would be ker-splat on the ground!

After we got so that she would move forward off my leg without trying to eat one of my feet, we had to deal with her neck muscles and canter. Her owner had held her head with the reins so that her muscles were more on the top of her neck instead of evenly spaced throughout her neck. She had a four beat canter instead of a three beat canter. Mr. Todden had me canter in long narrow figure eight patterns so she would pick up the lead on the curve and it would be the correct 3 beat canter. It smoothed out and Mr. Todden taught me to ride an English saddle and how to manage the double bit bridle. The snaffle bit is for lateral moves, like guiding. The curb bit was to set her head.

I got good enough in my English saddle that my feet stayed in the stirrup on the judge's side. When the canter was called for, my foot came out of the outside stirrup. I am certain the judge never knew. I really am a western kind of girl!

Dixie and I got so that we nearly always placed in the small town saddle club shows. We showed English and Western pleasure. In the Western pleasure classes, if the judge was partial to quarter horses, we got beat out of the first couple of places. If the judge was partial to Saddlebred horses, we usually won the class. Our entire horse world was made up of ponies, quarter horses and Saddlebred horses. I don't know when I saw my first Arabian, Morgan or thoroughbred horse. I knew about Tennessee

Walking Horses as we did encounter those horses at the Iowa State Fair Society Horse Shows.

I started riding Dixie everywhere. I rode on gravel roads and in the show ring. A teen-age girl, a natural horsemanship trainer and her beloved horse – there is not much better than that for a nervous Saddlebred. The next little girl that owned Dixie got a great horse. Was her life as wonderful as when I had her? Did she have any foals? Is there a piece of Dixie Lee Stonewall that is living today? Yo Saddlebred people: "Look her up in the registry and let me know!"

Horse Genes Goes Dormant

My life with horses stopped at age 18 when I went away to college. I knew what I wanted to do. In high school, I played Sports. Iowa was a State that believed in girls' athletics. I played professional high school basketball. Iowa loves girls' basketball! We had six girls on a team. Because there was this belief that girls might lose their reproductive organs by running too far or too fast, we had limits. We were limited to two dribbles and couldn't cross the center line. The points I scored in my high school basketball career are still in the middle of the top 100 girl athletes from Osceola. I still am on the record books in the 60 Yard Dash in track. While my father was living through pony-hell caring for the ponies in the awful cold, snowy, freezing and rainy Iowa winters, I practiced and played basketball.

I was wondering what the heck I wanted to be when I grew up. I noticed that the physical education teacher got to play all day long. That was the life for me! I was determined to have a career where I got to play.

College at Iowa State was great. I graduated from college with my Bachelor of Science degree in "play". The college job market was advertising for a physical education teacher in Milwaukee, Wisconsin for more money than anywhere else. I immediately filled out and application and was accepted. I was set for a life of play!

I arrived in Milwaukee and discovered that my junior high school was in the middle of a ghetto. No problem for me. I had no idea about the real world.

I had a few days to spend before the first day of school. There was this big frenzy going on in Chicago. I decided to drive to Chicago and see what the 1968 Democratic Riots were all about. There were 20,000 protestors and 30,000 police and military forces. The protestors rioted in downtown Chicago right where President Obama made his acceptance speech for president in 2010. I watched long-haired people getting clubbed and felt the burn of tear gas. The world changed. I was living in a police state with busloads of military and police forces everywhere. My Iowa life was a distant memory.

I returned to Milwaukee and entered my school. My gym classes numbered 50 to hundred girls. I had a home room and a health class. Many of my students could not read. If they could read, it was very slow. At the start of the second semester, I was given a modern math class to teach. "But wait," I said. "I didn't take math in college and I have no idea what modern math is. Their answer was desperate. "We have no one to teach this class. Take on the class and watch the education channel on TV. It has a weekly modern math course." Being a first year teacher in a ghetto junior high school didn't go very well for me. I was pretty mad at the world for allowing a ghetto to happen and children raised without being able to read. I made it eight months of the school year. I ran away to Chicago. My parents finally found me and came and got me. I volunteered to check in at a hospital in Des Moines with a mental ward. My condition was diagnosed as emotionally disturbed. Boy Howdy! What twenty two year old from a small Iowa town wouldn't have been emotionally disturbed!

I had fun in the hospital and my emotional health returned. When wellness returned, I applied and was selected for a job with Social Services in Chicago. I got to visit people in their homes. My case load area was the south side of Chicago. I got to visit with aged people and those with dependent children. Word on the street about me was good. No one in those days messed with the visiting social worker. We brought good to people.

One of my co-workers applied for a job with a federal agency and got a higher paying job. I applied and was selected for the same job. I got married and had a most wonderful young son. That marriage didn't work, and my son and I transferred to small Iowa town near where my parents lived.

I got married again and had a great small town Iowa life. My son had two great sets of grandparents. I was driven to better myself and after about eight years, I ended up in Kansas City. Again the marriage went bad. After a few years of being single, I found the man I'm married to today. We lived a good life in the city. In between my young life with horses and my old life with horses, I had three marriages, three careers and four relocations! That's quite a record.

My son went off to college and became an opera star. Yes, an opera star. We are not a musical family. We never heard him sing alone until he was a senior in high school. Then he blew everyone away with the lead role in a youth musical at the Village Presbyterian Church. Wowsa! His voice is a gift from God. He has performed all over the world and is still a most humble and fun wonderful son. Look him up at www.nathangranner.com. Listen to him on YouTube!

I'm still employed with that same agency and have over 40 years on the job. I couldn't ask for a better career.

BABY BOOMER WITH HORSE GENES

I entered second adulthood. I had given up on ever getting back into horses when suddenly my husband and I lost our minds. He wanted room to restore pickup trucks and John Deere tractors. I wanted a horse. We sold the house on which the mortgage was but 3 years from being paid off. We bought a house and acreage in the country. We became soundly saddled in debt and loving every minute. Naturally, the first thing I thought about was horse! I've had a 35 year gap. I last had a horse in 1964. Now we are in the year 1995.

We moved in November, and I had the sense to wait until the next spring / summer to get my horse. Now I had to decide what kind of a horse to get. I knew quarter horses and American Saddlebreds. What kind of horse would be for me? I dislike the quarter horse pleasure class with dead looking things, noses dragging on ground, but quarter horses could be fun in other areas. I loved my beautiful heads-up American Saddlebred, but I did not have much fun just being in pleasure saddle classes. I remember how high spirited she was too! I remember her jumping straight up and straight sideways. That was a scary thought.

I loved those racing events-pole bending and barrel racing in my youth. Did I want to go 100 mph with my very own racing quarter horse? No indeed!

I had a good friend with western pleasure quarter horses and a daughter who loved barrel racing. I asked her for advice to find a horse.

Here is her advice: "Buy a 10-12 year old gelding that has done many things." Today, we translate that as a been-there-done-that horse. Ha! I knew better than that. Didn't I show as a youth? Yes. Didn't I have a wonderful trainer? Yes. Didn't I remember lots of stuff? (Well, no, but that was a minor issue.) I would be bored with someone else's trained horse. I love to train horses and I want to start my own horse. No one else's problems or boring old horse for me! My husband was the only person who supported my decision. He knew less about horses than I did!

The world of horses changed quite a bit between 1964 and 1995! We fed our horses oats back then. Oats came from the feed store. We had our loose oats delivered into our feed room. We did not worm horses. Horses were old around 16 or 17. The new world got technology and changed. Horse feed had been invented. I was to learn that the horse genes dictate that you use the money from your job to live your dream with horses.

I looked in the paper and went to visit one or two people who had a horse for sale. Nothing seemed right and I wasn't even motivated to ride these horses.

CONCERT OF CHAMPIONS
AMERICAN ROYAL 1995

It was a black tie event. The Kansas City Chamber Orchestra played while different horses and horse acts performed at the American Royal Kemper Arena. The orchestra was dressed fancy. It was advertised fancy. The affair was advertised all over the Kansas City newspapers. It was a horse event and I had to go. I need to learn all about horses before I make my choice of which horse to buy.

I arrived and bought my ticket. This concert is where I mysteriously discovered the Missouri Fox Trotter horse. It was a gift from God.

I got my ticket and went into the huge arena with seats that go up into the nosebleed sky. Everyone was seated in the two middle sections and the sections were crammed full of people. My seat was in another section. This section had exactly one person in it and my seat was next to this person. One person seated in the midst of 200 seats. "Odd," I thought. "Very odd." I climbed up a number of stairs, suffered a little vertigo when I looked down in the arena. I sat down next to a 30 something year old man. We spoke and then the horse event started. It was lovely indeed with fancy horses doing wondrous things.

Into the arena came three beautiful horses. In danced the gorgeous Missouri Fox Trotters with their smooth gait and their long flowing manes and tails. I sat up. They were doing the oddest gait. Their heads were nodding. Their tails were waving like flags and the riders were sitting completely still in total comfort. There was no bouncing of a human being body part in that arena! I was amazed.

The horses and riders rode around the arena while the onlookers gawked. The announcer told the crowd that these were world champion horses and riders. My mouth was gap-jawed in astonishment. The horses left the arena and there was a little bit of time between "acts". Turns out my "seat mate" knew all about Missouri Fox Trotters as he grew up in the Ozarks. He joyfully described the comfortable gait and how laid back these fox trotters were. I was thinking these horses must be really expensive and I asked how much they went for. He explained, "Missouri Fox Trotters are very reasonably priced. They are horses for regular folks, not fancy arena horses. The silver tack in horse shows is discouraged as these horses want to prove what great smooth rides they are without excessive outlay of money for silver adornment. These are horses developed in the Ozark region of Missouri. Ozark people did not have money for silver. They just wanted a great smooth horse that could do everything." "Wow!" I thought.

Here's the meant-to-be story. This total stranger was placed solo in a seating section of around 200 seats so that I could sit beside him and learn about the existence of Missouri Fox Trotters with their wonderful laid-back character and their smooth traveling gait. They had the long manes of tails of a Saddlebred and the calm manner of a quarter horse. This was my horse!

Just recently I learned the riders were Geno Middleton, Doug Williams and Patty Donley. They were riding World Grand Champions. Geno is the third generation of World Championship professional trainers. He's won more championships than anyone else living or deceased in Missouri Fox Trotter horse shows. Patty Donley has gone on to horse heaven. Her friends mourn her greatly and her show life with Missouri Fox Trotters will be remembered by many.

That's how I made the decision to get a Missouri Fox Trotter as my horse. I knew no one who had fox trotters and the Internet wasn't even in my vocabulary yet. That was 1995.

Bad Decision Made My Dream Come True

One day I woke up and found a newspaper mention of a colt start demonstration. This was back when natural horsemanship had just started. I went to the demonstration. Who it was, I don't remember, but I was impressed. I knew this was the real deal, and it was for me. All you need is a round pen and the ability to determine when the horse is ready to "join up" with the human. The demonstrator took us from a two-year-old horse that was leery of people and finishing up with riding the horse around with a saddle.

The horse was pretty determined not to join up with the trainer. The trainer kept telling us that at any moment, the horse would turn into the middle and "face up". It took so long that I had made bets with my fellow watchers. I bet the person sitting next to me $1.00 that the horse would never do anything but try to run away from the trainer.

After a long while, the horse turned into the center and faced the trainer. We went longer and longer and the horse became tamer and tamer. Finally, he was a nice tame horse, not bothered by anything in the area. The trainer saddled the horse and dealt with the scary girth. At the end of the demonstration, the trainer was riding the horse.

I was sold. I needed a round pen before I got my horse. Soon after that, I discovered John Lyon's "Round Pen Reasoning" book. I got the book and read it about 5 times. I bought the video and watched it twice. I was ready for my first horse! What with my prior experience with Mr. Todden, Dr. Paul and Austin Smith along with my childhood riding experiences, I would be galloping with Roy Rogers and Gene Autry.

Yee Haw

Thus I ignored the advice of knowledgeable horse people. Other people in the horse world had told me to find the mythical 12-year-old gelding that had "been there and done that". Sheesh! I needed a young unstarted horse! I needed a two-year-old Missouri Fox Trotter!

PRETTY HORSES —SOLD!

In the 90's, we had no Internet. We had newspaper classifieds. We had post-it boards at local stores. That is how we bought and sold stuff. That was our world.

I had no idea who those people were at the American Royal with their Fox Trotters. I had no idea we had a Kansas City Fox Trotter club. I had no human source to find my dream horse.

I found a business card at a local store post-it board that gave a name, telephone number and these magic words, *"Fox Trotters for Sale"*. I called and drove fifty miles to meet Bob and MaryMae Lewis in Butler, Mo. MaryMae sent me out into the farmyard where Bob and another man were looking at the most beautiful horse I've ever seen! She was in a round pen. We were staring at her. I told Bob that I was looking for a fox trotter to buy. I said, "I love this horse right here". We chatted a moment and I discovered that this gorgeous dark grey creature was a mare, two years old and unstarted. I also discovered that the other man had already bought her! Clearly, this guy knew I was destined to be the next world champion Missouri Fox Trotter owner. He said, "I'll let you have this horse."

Turns out the man was buying most of Bob's two-year-old horses. He had a local trainer ride these two year olds. He put them in a trailer, drove them to Arizona or California, and sold them for a lot more money than he gave Bob. Missouri Fox Trotters were a rare commodity in those two states. I thanked the man with much gratitude. Bob and I settled on a price. I think it was $1200. Bob made more money selling me the horse. That was the real reason why the man let me have her. He was buying horses at a bulk rate.

At the time, I thought I needed my husband's approval to buy this horse. I drove fifty miles back home to find my husband had just returned from a trip searching for tractors fifty miles north of where we lived. I was practically spitting in hysterical news! "I found my horse! I want you to come to Butler and approve! We are leaving now!"

On the way there, I broached the subject of horses being a herd animal. I explained to my husband that one horse would be lonely and that I really needed two horses. I knew Bob had yearlings. I told my husband that I needed the gray horse with whom I fell in love. I told him that I also needed a black horse. I've always loved black horses and it would remind me of Cricket, my black Shetland pony. In my youth watching the society horse shows, occasionally I saw a black American Saddlebred. Those black Saddlebreds were the most beautiful! I told the spouse that I would bargain with Bob and get two horses for a nice price.

My husband and Bob liked each other a lot. They were both "good ole boys". Terry saw that the creature I had fallen in love with was a horse. She was able to walk around. She was breathing. He gave his approval. I told Bob that I needed another horse, a black yearling filly.

Bob packed us into this 1970 rattle pickup truck and drove us down the road to a 40 acre pasture. We drove out into the pasture searching for the yearling herd. There they were! We drove close to the herd and got out. Bob thought maybe we would spook them and they would run away. We drove up and twenty horses picked up their heads and looked at us. Instead of running away, the yearling fox trotter herd came over and sniffed us out. Bob had three black filly yearlings. He asked me if I wanted the black horse with the prettiest head. "Absolutely!" I said. " I love pretty heads on horses!" Bob went into the herd and examined all three black heads. He announced the winner. I accepted his $900 price on the spot. Forget that bargaining thing. I had a black horse with a beautiful head!

Bob's next job was to deliver the horses! He had to get two horses, not trained to lead, to load into a trailer and deliver them to my house. And he did! It's good that I didn't have to watch that trailer loading into a small two horse trailer.

We had a horse warming party. A bunch of my friends greeted the most beautiful gray and the most beautiful black horse to their new home. We were able to lead them into the pasture. The black horse stayed around and accepted carrots and apples. The gray horse left the party. We could see her now and then. She did not go too far away from the black horse who was still slurping up her new treats and enjoying being petted. Then we had a picnic and I basked in the knowledge that I was a horse owner. My horse genes were overjoyed.

The gray horse's registered name was Trixie. I knew she was not a Trixie personality. Since her famous bloodlines were Zane Grey and my favorite western writer of all time was Zane Grey, I named her after his most famous book, **Riders of the Purple Sage**. Her name became Zane Gray Purple Sage. That was so original. It took me months to come up with that name!

The black horse's name was Glory Bee. Yeccha to that name! I wanted a name befitting her Toddy Perfection bloodlines and her wonderful black color. After many months searching for the perfect name, her registered name changed to Toddy's Velvet Perfection.

Velvet and Sage had come into my life. My life as a beginning adult rider with a yearling and an unstarted two-year-old was about to begin. My horse genes could barely wait to start galloping over the Missouri hills.

ROUND PEN RODEO

Here are the round pen rules per John Lyons. The horse is out on the edge of the round pen circle. The human is in the middle. There are no ropes. This is called "liberty". Once the horse wants to be with the human, the horse gets to rest in the middle with the human. If the horse gets bothered by what the human does, the horse gets to go out at a trot or canter on the circle again until desensitization occurs and the horse can handle resting in the middle. If the horse is out on the circle and turns to face you, the horse deserves a break of some kind.

The horse must show that he wants to be with you, even follow you while you walk around.

Desensitizing musts:

The human must be able to touch a relaxed horse anywhere. It doesn't count if the horse doesn't like being touched, but resists running away to the perimeter of the circle. The horse has to be relaxed wherever it is touched…even where the apples go in and come out (mouth and rear end expulsion part).

The human must be able to approximate sounds, actions and situations that might spook a horse in an arena, out on the trail, at a circus, at a carnival, in a parade and on a cattle drive. Of course, most of that simulation is not possible, but what we want is a horse that thinks and realizes that out of place noises, objects and sounds will not kill the horse. When a horse spooks, the horse is thinking about being killed. Running is the flight response built into a horse. This is not a pleasant occurrence for a trail rider or a rider in any kind of sport. When horses bolt, usually the human falls off. All riders hate to fall off because it hurts. Riders hate to be on a bolting horse because all control is lost. It feels like you are going 100 mph and are probably going to meet a semi-truck head-on. It is terrifying.

Thankfully I could trap Sage out in the big pasture so could lead her into the round pen. I turned her loose. She was aloof and ignored me. Our first task was for her to want to be with me. Sage thought being outside the round pen running loose in the pasture was a much better deal. Instead of looking at me, she looked outside the round pen into her beloved pasture.

True to John Lyon's teaching, Sage did much running around the round pen. She stopped. She turned out on the circle and ran the other way. It took quite a while to get her to face into the circle to turn. That's OK. I knew that I wasn't going to ride Sage the first week. After all, I was new to this concept.

Sage and I spent a lot of time in the round pen before I convinced her that she wanted to stand next to me in the center. She did learn that the center was a place of rest. She liked that part a lot.

Sage's desensitization started. I need to touch her everywhere. Sage didn't like me to touch her anywhere. She didn't want me to touch her head. Touching her stomach was out of the question. Touching her tail head was outrageous. Picking up her feet was not an option. Whenever Sage strongly objected to anything, she was sent out to run around the round pen. When she decided to allow me to touch her in the "new spot", she came back into the middle, got to rest and be petted. I had to win each spot on her body. The days flew into weeks.

Remember the trainer who did the colt start demo? He was saddling that horse in about 2 hours. It took Sage a lot longer before we got to the saddle part. The saddle pad took about two days. Sage became a very physically fit horse. She got to canter for long periods of time every day.

One day I walked out to the horse pasture and I saw Sage and Velvet in the round pen. I left the gate open, so they can have access. Sage was in the middle and Velvet was running around on the perimeter. Velvet stopped and Sage ran at her with ears back and teeth barred. Velvet took off running. I witnessed this four more times. Velvet tried to stop and Sage ran at her. As soon as Velvet was running around, Sage just stood in the middle. I was astounded. Sage was playing the round pen game with Velvet. Sage was the boss and Velvet wasn't. I could see that Velvet was frustrated. She was getting tired. She would have gladly come into the middle with Sage, but Sage wasn't having it. Finally Velvet stopped and laid down. Sage ran at her, but Velvet stayed on the ground. That was the only way that Velvet got to stop and rest. Sage had become an accomplished round pen trainer!

Finally the big day had come. Sage was ready for the saddle. I had the husband come out to the round pen. He was going to see Sage with a saddle on. Excitement reverberated through my whole being. I was near ready to be galloping over hill and dale like Roy Rogers and Trigger!

I put the saddle on. I tightened up the cinch. I took off her halter. Sage was "at liberty"! Spouse and I were watching her. I was proud of her. I sent her out on the circle. As Sage picked up a little speed. she discovered that she was trapped inside a saddle! Right in front of our eyes, she turned into a rodeo bucking horse. She exploded straight up. She started to run and buck. The frightened spouse started to run. He took off out on the circle too. I had a husband and a bucking monster running around the round pen. Both of them were certain death was coming!

I screamed at the spouse. "Get into the center! Come in here with me!" He did not know the rule about center being the safe spot and the fence being the run-around part. He ran into the center still convinced that he was going to be trampled. Sage stayed on the circle, calmed down her bucking and ran around for a while. Finally, she stopped and came into the center. The spouse calmed down and escaped from the round pen. That was a three wine bottle evening! My spouse had three wines and I had three wines. This might have been when my husband first had doubts that I was a master trainer.

GREEN ON GREEN IS BLACK AND BLUE

Horse trainer proud is what I felt like the next day. I flipped that saddle on Sage. She ran around the circle for a while. There was no bucking, just a nice calm horse. I put the bridle with the John Lyons recommended bit on her. John Lyons recommended a certain snaffle bit and I made certain I had that exact bit in her mouth. I did some practice on the ground to see if she would turn her head with the bit in her mouth.

Ready to ride was I. I did ride and it went well. I got on her and we walked around the round pen both ways. Yee Haw! I was thrilled. I got off. I rode the 2nd day at a walk both ways of the round pen and it went well.

I would be cantering soon over Missouri hilly terrain. On the third day of riding, Trainer Susan called husband out to see her ride. I was sitting on Sage all glorious. I was showing the husband that I was a master horse trainer. I noticed some of her mane was all jumbled up with her forelock in the top of the bridle. I reached down to straighten out the forelock and mane.

Here's how spouse describes it: "Sage turned three circles. Susan turned two circles." I had never touched Sage's head from on top of anything. She spooked and whirled at the touch. I stayed with her for two of the three circles and then centrifugal force threw me off and I hit the hard cruel ground.

Ker-SPLAT!
"waves of pain"
"more waves of pain"
"was I broken?"

Maybe childbirth hurt worse, but at least I was drugged. It was totally shocking how much that hurt. I don't ever remember falling off a horse in my young days. I'm 48 years old with all this fat weight. The law of physics stated that the meeting of my body and the ground would be shockingly painful. No, I didn't get back on and ride. I took off the bridle, saddle and limped back to the house. I didn't know it at the time, but that set up the chain of events that led me to the Parelli system of training, Jennifer Vaught and my wonderful life with horses.

MY NEW EXTENDED FAMILY

After my sore and aching body rested a bit, husband and I discussed the sudden evaporation of my horse trainer ability. I spoke heatedly, "I need to find a young person to ride this horse! Let's get me a young person, like a cowboy. This cowboy can just get on Sage and ride until she gets used to stuff. Then I can start riding her." Husband thought this was a fine idea. The thought of me spending months in a plaster cast with a couple of broken limbs was not a pleasant thought for the husband. I am certain he might have thought about how miserable his life would be as my servant. The search for a cowboy began.

I found someone thru the classified. We went to visit him. He was a pleasant person and I hired him to ride Sage. At work, the husband was telling his friends about this. One of his co-workers had heard of this man and the story was not good. I believe the story was "cruel". I called the cowboy and *unhired* him. I lied and said someone closer and a good friend was discovered who did this kind of stuff.

We found someone else and he was hired. Sage would be ridden out in the country fields. All was well. The deal was made for the beginning of the next month.

It was a photocopied faded poster at the grocery store that came at the right time. The poster said, Natural Horsemanship Clinic – come and audit. It's this coming weekend. I called the phone number and drove over to meet my future home-away-from-home and my new extended family.

I went to Pine Dell Farm and met Dale. She was selling tickets to the clinic. I was introduced to Ed Moulis, owner of Pine Dell. Ed has never known a stranger. In fact, when you are introduced to Ed, you instantly become bonded to him. It is uncanny. He has this ability to instantly become your best and most trusted friend.

Dale told me about Jenny Vaught, the trainer. She said that Jenny understands horses so well, she acts instinctively with the horse. "Jenny is half horse", said Dale. I thought that was pretty cool. I was meeting a half horse kind of a person!

I met Jenny. We all chatted. I liked her a lot. I bought the ticket to the clinic and went out to my locked car. Sadly, the keys were in the ignition. I was so excited to be at Pine Dell Farm that I accidentally locked the doors when I got out. "Dale, I've locked myself out." "No problem, Susan. We'll just get Ed." I might have really like Ed the first time I met him, but when he came to unlock my door, it was instant adoration. Ed has been my boyfriend ever since. He told me that in the running of Pine Dell Farm, he has gotten just as good as any car thief in the instant unlocking of car doors.

My hero!

NOSE TO NOSE WITH NATURAL HORSEMANSHIP

Your everyday basic beginning Parelli Level 1 clinic is what I walked into. I was blind and then I wasn't. It was a two-day clinic. Lee Smith was the Parelli Certified Instructor. She grabbed my attention and never let it go. I can barely explain what the Parelli seven games are so that non-Parelli people have an understanding. They are the seven yields along with horsemanship based on psychology of communicating with another species, the horse! Lee explained this thoroughly while I watched the 15 horses and people go through the class. "Oh my goodness" as we say when we can't find any other words! The Round Pen Reasoning with John Lyons was but a tiny slice of the picture. The Parelli system takes you from the very start of understanding horses and takes you baby step thru baby step up to my dream of riding with Roy Rogers and Trigger.

This is a method based on safety for everyone. This is bonding of horse and human. Oh the joy! I took tons of notes. I wrote down everything Lee Smith said. I never looked at my notes again. Instead, I learned everything she said in the years to come up until the present day.

After the day was over, I went over to Jenny and asked her to start Velvet in the next three months, a little before she turned age two. Jenny was a certified Parelli instructor and trained horses and people at Pine Dell Farm. This stable is six miles from where I live. Oh Joy.

I still didn't get the whole picture. Thankfully, my farrier helped me out.

John Sitter was hunched over trimming Sage's feet. I went on and on about what I had experienced with Lee Smith and the Parelli natural horsemanship philosophy. I told him that I had already hired a person to take Sage, but I was conflicted with wanting Sage to be trained by Jenny instead. I had a sense of rightness and wrongness. I had made a deal with the other trainer.

John said, "Have Jenny train Sage". "What?" I said. "But I already made the deal." John repeated himself, "Have Jenny train Sage." "But, but, I hate confrontation." John said, "Have Jenny train Sage". I obeyed.

Thank God! Thank you John Sitter!

Sage went to Jenny and Pine Dell shortly thereafter. I started taking lessons with Karen, Jenny's mother. I got to ride a lesson horse. Karen coached me in the seven games riding an experienced horse. One of the mottos that Parelli lives by is "Horses teach riders and riders teach horses." Guess who was teaching who in this stage of my journey? Karen took me through all the ground games. When I first got on the horse, Karen held the lead rope attached to the halter. We walked around and my body started thinking it was pretty darn safe up there. My body relaxed. Oh my. Riding horses might be just a lot of fun. My horse genes agreed!

Lesson Horse "Heaven for Beginners"

The Parelli method and Karen Moulis put together makes for a fine foundation of horsemanship. Karen makes horse-riding fun. She keeps you feeling safe until you are ready to cross the fear threshold. She has great lesson horses.

I was kept on a 22' rope while riding and Karen had me doing various exercises cleverly designed to help me my balance on a horse. The day came when I got to be in control of the horse and that was great. The 22' rope came off and I was responsible for the reins. I grew to love my lesson horse. He kept me safe. He was Jenny's Parelli Levels horse, Sasha. When we say, this is my "Levels' Horse", it means, the horse we are taking through Level 1 and on. Your "Levels' Horse" is your main ride. Learning the psychology of communication with the horse, feel and balance dictates that you spend a lot of time with your "Levels' Horse".

In the Parelli method, we learn to stop, turn and back by weight shifts and heel pressure (in the horse world, we call that "leg aides"). We learn the direct rein and the indirect rein. We learn how to move the front and back parts of the horse. We learn to focus. Everything that you learn is contrary to human natural instincts. Our instinct is to look down at our horse and move our hands very fast. Instead, one must look where the horse is to go and have slow moving hands.

Karen has a lot of fun teaching. I swear she could correct me for the same body position failure 50 times and pretend as if it was the first time she had told me. Years and years later, I still have Karen talking in my head when my focus or weight shift is wrong. She will live forever in that portion of my brain. Her voice has become my instinct.
"Look up and sit back for the direct rein (horse moves the front feet)."

"Look back at the horse's rear and shift weight forward for the indirect rein (horse moves their hind legs)."

"Look up where you are going. You don't need to watch your horse's ears."

I became Karen's star pupil. You need not mention this to any of her other students. All Karen's students feel like a star pupil. We discussed me practicing for the Level 1 Parelli test. Since I had a horse in training with Jenny, Karen decided I could use a lesson horse and practice on my own for the Level 1 tasks. Whoopee! I forget that horse's name. We were well underway. I was playing with and riding a safe horse. That's exactly what I was doing when Jenny spoke the unexpected. I guess that I understood that Sage was being trained by Jenny so that I could ride her. But the fear from that "Ker-Splat" action made my brain block out the thought that I would eventually ride Sage. That concept had left my brain in my joy with the lesson horse. Ride Sage? Egad!

SAGE IS READY FOR YOU TO RIDE

"Sage is ready for you to ride her." After Jenny first started Sage, I watched them play the ground games in the round pen and was impressed. What we train is building a relationship and response to "feel". Do not feel bad if you don't understand the term "response to feel". I just made it up and besides it took me about 7-8 years to understand what "feel" really is between horse and human.

Jenny trained during the day. I came to Pine Dell after work. Somehow, I did not bother to ask for any special showing of Jenny riding Sage. It probably slipped out of my mind because my mind was filled with Riding-Sage-Fear! My mind kept that a secret from me. My brain and I avoided thinking about riding Sage.

"Sage is ready for you to ride her." Those words shelved me getting to use the Pine Dell Lesson horse to pass the Level 1 test. I had a horse of my own to ride. Gulp!

The deal is that the owner of a horse in training gets to have a weekly lesson with Jenny. She told me that the time had come. Big Gulp, but I was confident and ready. That's what I thought!

Sage and I met after two months of separate training. I was not scared of the gentle lesson horses, but this was something else again. I mounted Sage and sat in the saddle looking like Dale Evans, a cowgirl.

Jenny told me to relax. I took a deep breath and relaxed. Jenny told me that I appeared to be standing in the saddle. She told me my knees were straight. I took a deep breath and relaxed even more. I told Jenny I was relaxed. Jenny tried to move my leg and bend my knee. My knee would not move. Maybe I wasn't relaxed. Jenny told me that my knees were locked and braced. I was really standing up in the saddle. I was rigid. Every muscle in my body was tight with fear and tension. My brain was lying to me. My brain told me that I was relaxed, but my body told Jenny that I was rigid.

Jenny asked me to give Sage a little leg pressure and ask her to move. Sage hated my frozen body. She refused to move, tried to bite my legs, and cow kicked. My immediate thought was, *"My life is over. Surely Jenny will take me off this creature! But no, Jenny was telling me to squeeze her with my legs, spank her rear with my hand, spank her rear with the lead rope. Finally, Sage made a step and we started all over again."*

I'm in hell!

Jenny talked me through this like the control tower in the movies helping the passenger land the airplane after the pilot dies. The only difference was that I wanted to be the dead pilot! About half way in this refusal to move forward, (we progressed about 5 yards), we started to move slowly around the arena with mad, disgruntled horse things happening. I think we almost made it one lap around the arena. I decided that I should cry because I was a tremulous mess. I needed to cry. I teared up and thought, *"I'm going to tell Jenny that I want off!"* But Jenny kept talking to me...talking me through every step. I had made one lap around the arena both ways. Finally the time was over. I got to dismount and I was alive! I was wringing wet with sweat. There were other people in the arena that night. I couldn't see them; I only sensed them!

They came over and told me I did really well. I was able to recognize them once I got off Sage. Jenny told me I did really well. I felt better, especially since my feet were on the ground. It was a three-wine-bottle celebration night.

The 2nd lesson, I was much more confident; but Sage was worse. She refused to move. She pinned her ears and kicked her back leg forward. I had to get off. Jenny got on, and made Sage very uncomfortable about not moving. Sage got to turn on her hindquarters with a lot of effort. That was not fun for Sage. I got back on again with more confidence and asked Sage to move forward. She did. It was a banner day. I continued to play ground games with Sage and had the weekly riding lesson with Jenny. I continued my lesson horse weekly session with Karen as well.

I got up the courage to ride Sage by myself in the round pen. That worked out really well. My next attempt would be to ride up in the Pine Dell 40 acres. I corralled someone and we went on my first ride outside the arena. Sage did excellent and I was very happy.

I remember riding Sage out in the 40 acres by myself. The sky was blue with a few white puffy clouds. Sage was perfect, and I was relaxed. "Riding Sage is fun!"

Life was good and then the stumbling started. The stumbling started when Sage began to pace. She took every opportunity to pace. Pace is moving the back legs and the front legs on the same side at the same time. It feels like riding a camel must feel. I'm a beginning adult rider with zilch for knowledge. I'm working on my leg aides, body shifts and focus. I really don't have the sophisticated knowledge about the gaits. As a matter of fact, I don't know anything about the gaits other than what I saw in the coliseum that night…smooth Missouri Fox Trotter horses nodding their heads with their tales waving like a flag.

Pacing horses have a tendency to stumble. They don't have to lift their feet very far off the ground. The hoof tip catches on the smallest of bump in the ground and they trip. It is not all that fun to ride a constantly tripping horse. It gives a rider the impression that the horse might trip and fall down. Riders hate the thought of meeting the ground. Beginning riders especially hate the thought that the horse will fall.

One day Sage and I were practicing in the smaller outdoor arena at Pine Dell. Sage tripped and fell to her knees. I was launched forward, over the saddle horn and landed on her neck. My feet remained in the stirrups. In fact, my boots would not leave the stirrups. My boots are stuck in the stirrups! My feet are stuck in the stirrups. I hung on Sage's neck with my face about a foot away from the dear ground. I was too heavy laying on her neck for her to get up. There Sage and I were, both of us unable to move. Finally, I wiggled my boots free of the stirrups and slithered to the ground. That was my best ever trip from saddle to the ground!

When I got back on Sage, I decided to cry for a while. The fear adrenalin was trying to leave my body. "Life wasn't fair. I had a Missouri Fox Trotter that didn't fox trot!" It scared me when she tripped to her knees. "Life wasn't fair. The world owes me a smooth fox trotter like I saw at the Concert of Champions!"

TRAIL RIDE LEARNING

About two months after I was able to ride Sage without much fear, I was talked into going to Eminence. Eminence is a place where you camp with your horse and ride out on trails. There are wild horses that live farther from the camp. Eminence is surrounded by the giant Mark Twain National Forest. You can ride for hours in this forest and never see another horse and rider. The person who talked me into going was the same knowledgeable person who told me I should buy the mythical been-there-done-that gelding. I had a lot of respect for her knowledge by then.

Sage, husband and I went on the weeklong Eminence Trail ride– in the Ozark Mountains with 4000+ other horses. My husband is a social person, not a rider. I intended to ride only in the parking lot and campground. But no my good friend told me after we got there, *"No-you're going on nice short daily trail rides. You can't come to Eminence and not ride! After you ride a week at Eminence everything else will be easy!"*

Sage did great. She wasn't scared of anything! She walked two inches beside clangorous diesel trucks. We rode around the campgrounds filled with horse eating things.

I was a nervous wreck the first morning and cried, making certain no one could see that I was crying. I had tears streaming down my face, but my face was absolutely frozen in a noncommittal nothing. I went for 15 or 20 minutes at a time holding my breath…maybe less. Sage and I did lots of groundwork to get me prepared for riding!

Out on the trail, we crossed water; we climbed hills. I survived! I didn't have fun, but it wasn't torture either. Every morning when I got up, I wondered if I'd be dead or disabled by the time the day's trail ride was over. I saw it as a 50-50 chance of survival. Sage was very sure-footed on the ride. She didn't stumble. She made certain her feet didn't trip.

We participated in an evening horse show with record number 60 horses in the arena at the same time. Other horses bucked and riders flew off in the overly crowded arena. Sage was great! Back at Pine Dell, we rode in many lessons in arenas with other horses. We had a lot of practice in the Parelli "squeeze game" that prepares the horse for a melee like this.

Here's what happened on the Wednesday trail ride:

We came to a river and two year old Sage was hot after climbing a steep horrid mountain. She went into the river a short distance to drink the water. She pawed the water to clear the dirt when my friend yelled at me. However, I was intently watching Sage's front leg sinking into a hole. It just seemed to sink down farther and farther. I was patiently waiting for her to pull her leg out of the hole when my friend's frantic voice yelled "JUMP OFF!" This was a very loud and demanding voice! My body responded just when Sage sank down on her belly. I leaped from the saddle into the shallow river! I got up and waited for Sage to get up.

"Quicksand," I was thinking when she didn't get up. *She's caught in quicksand!"* I was running in circles around her in the water around her trying to figure out how to get her out of the quicksand when my friend's voice penetrated my brain again. *"Slap her; Yell at her! She's going to roll!"* "Roll"? I thought.*"Not quicksand?"* I yelled, jumped and flapped my arms which caused Sage to heave herself to her feet.

I got a lecture about sweaty horses and pawing water! Oh, she lay down in the cool river because she was hot and sweaty! That leg thing was her folding her front leg when she first started to lay down. Good GAD! Who would have thought!

I couldn't mount my horse without a big natural mounting block and none was available. My friend had to get off her horse, kneel with one leg and put my muddy wet foot on her thigh so that I could heave myself on Sage. My jeans from knees down were sopping wet and 20 pounds heavier. Grunt and on the horse I was. We made it across the river and I started thinking about our water adventure when we came to the part of the trail that was deep warm sand. . . .

Without any warning, PLUNK!...down we went. It was a broken record. No slouch in the learning not-to-die-experience, I was smart enough to leap off as we were going down. I dove into the deep sand in my sopping wet jeans...100 more pounds packed on my body. Sage wanted to lie down and roll in the sand to dry up her sweaty hair. I lurched to my feet and stopped Sage from rolling in the sand. Now I have 100 lbs. more weight with the wet sand sticking to my jeans. The emotional devastation took every source of strength from my body. I was saved by my friend's husband who had come to join us. It took all his strength to hoist my weak, quivering, dead weight body back on Sage.

On the way back to camp, a wide river crossing had to be negotiated. Everyone rode very close to Sage ready to beat her if she even blinked a lie-down eye! I felt like a steer herded by cowboy drovers!

Oh trail riding is really, really fun!

I wrote Jenny a thank you card after I recovered from Eminence. I discovered that trail horses need all the foundation skills that a Jenny Vaught trained horse has. Sometimes you are walking along thru a dense forest on a trail and the trail disappears, leaving you hip to hip with dense trees and brush. Turning around is not an option unless you want to take out a few trees and shrubs. Backing up to a turnaround spot is heaven. "Thank you for teaching Sage how to back." Getting those front legs to circle around a muddy puddle is Cadillac trail riding. "Thank you for the turn on the hind quarters." Going along a forest trail has trees that are placed just perfect to take off your knee. "Thank you for the making Sage's hindquarters movable." I dodged the knee-eating trees. "Thank you, Jenny for training Sage how to sidepass." We sidepassed over to big tree trunks and big rocks so I could dismount and mount in ease.

"Thank you, Jenny Vaught, for the training of my wonderful two-year-old Sage!"

TRAIL RIDE TO FEAR

Thursday was the start of the year of *"downhill"* fear. My friend erred in judgment and took me up and down a mountainous steep hill where the path consisted of rock ledges littered with loose rocks. Going up was frightening but the descent was beyond agony. I was frozen with fear going down. When I expressed some verbal dismay to my friend, she told me just to relax and lean back! HA! We did make it down alive, and even though I'm not a Catholic, I did the Cross Gesture! I couldn't get off to kiss the ground because I couldn't easily mount my horse and we were still miles away from the campground.

After we got back and I had semi recovered, my friend's husband took me aside and had a little talk with me. *"I am really worried about you and your "little, slight fox trotter! If only you had purchased a blocky horse—like a quarter horse. I'm certain there must be blocky fox trotters that could handle your weigh, but Sage isn't strong enough to handle your weight on these Ozark Mountains. If Sage would have tripped up there on the mountain and started to fall, she couldn't have recovered. You need a blocky horse."*

Instant Bad Brain Image: I imagined that horrid ride down the loose rocky ledges, Sage and I falling. Sage with bones sticking up out of her. Sage dead of a broken neck. Susan with a broken neck lying on Sage's broken legs. Those images flashed through my brain.

THE BIG FEAR OF DOWNHILL hit me like a sledge hammer. I managed to contain the fear so no one else knew.

Sage, the two-year-old, wasn't afraid of anything in that camp of 4000 horses! Susan, the 49 year old, turned into a battered shell with zero confidence. I made up some excuse, and we left the next morning.

I was able to ride Sage around my property and the neighboring turf farm because it is mostly flat. I couldn't ride through the shallow ditches to get from the pasture to the road. I had to find a crossing place that was flat.

I was so proud of Sage. She is not scared of anything in the world! This is when she started earning the nickname, *"Sage the Brave"*. At home we were zipping by some bushes and heard a "lion rattle sound". Without my permission, Sage took her saddle and leaped ahead about 5 feet. However, my body did not travel with the saddle. You know those cartoon characters that run off a cliff. "HUH…there's only daylight underneath me," and…thud. I met the unforgiving ground again! I had to lay there for a while waiting for the intense pain to go away. After my tremulous mass of flesh calmed down, I determined that I was not broken.

I was too hurt to climb back on that day. Riding was only pretend after that. It was too cold, too late, too hot, I felt too bad. Winter came…no riding and I was grateful. Now I had the downhill fear plus the ker-splat fear again.

I gave Sage back to Jenny for 3-4 more months of training. I kept on taking lessons with Karen. When horses were in training with Jenny, you also got a half hour lesson with Jenny weekly. I was taking 1 ½ hours of lessons every week.

Here's what I was left with in my 1st Year with Horses:

DOWNHILL FEAR: If the ground were sloped enough so a golf ball would roll downhill, I was major scared.

RIDING DREAD (RD) That's when all the excuses for not riding are made. It's a disease called RD!

It took me at least a year to get over my downhill fear. I couldn't cross ditches. I had to find flat places to ride. Pine Dell has a nice slight hill from the barns up to the 40 acres. Most people wouldn't call it a hill. I was able to easily make it up to the 40 acres, but coming down was different. I was convinced that Sage would fall. Her feet probably would slide out from under her, and she and I would go crashing down. No one noticed that I got off Sage to walk down the hill. It was a nice gesture for me to make for Sage. She got to eat some grass and then we walked down to the barns and my trailer.

Gradually with time, my fears left. I became able to cross a ditch. I made the final experiment going down a steep hill riding bareback. I wasn't scared. I turned the corner on the downhill fear!

Riding lessons with Karen and Jenny increased my confidence again. My riding balance improved. The Ker-splat fear left again.

Firecracker Clinic

Parelli Instructor, David Lichman, came to Pine Dell Farm to give a Level 1 clinic. David Lichman's background is the Tennessee Walking Horse world. He rode a horse to a world grand championship. Jenny also rode a Tennessee Walking horse to many championships, both in Missouri and the World Celebration. These two people knew gaited horses.

One afternoon, David and Jenny watched me ride Sage in the arena. They watched her pace and occasionally get a few steps at the smooth running walk. I had whined that I bought a fox trotter and wanted her to fox trot. They counseled me on the great smoothness of the running walk. That is what I was going to get with Sage someday and I should be grateful for it.

Sigh. That was before we all realized that riding gaited horses is a "master class". Beginning riders don't have the feel, the timing and the knowledge of the horse to affect the gait. Riding with the Parelli methods is 80% loose reins and beginners are just learning to stay on the up side of the horse. I could feel the camel feeling of the pace and the occasional smoothness of the running walk.

It was very hot for that clinic. It was a three-day clinic and we had a fantastic time. On the last day late in the afternoon, David Lichman decided on the last task of the seven games. The task is "controlled catastrophe". When your horse gets scared of something, the danger is that the horse will turn and bolt in fear. Riding a bolting horse is a recipe for impending death. No one enjoys riding a galloping totally-out-of-control horse. The secret is to keep the horse facing the danger. We use the reins to keep the horse's head straight. Turning away from the scary object is the death sentence. The horse is allowed to back as far as they want away from the scary object, but has to keep facing the object.

David had us all form a large circle with him in the middle. Dusk was not far away. He fumbled around in his pocket and pulled out a firecracker and a lighter. What HO! As we all watched in horrified fascination, he lit the firecracker and tossed it a few feet away from him. POP!!! Some of the horses moved, but not Sage. He pulled out another firecracker and lit it. Another and another firecracker he lit. Most of the horses were now able to stand and watch. Sage had not moved.

Here's the part where Sage finally earned her name. David had a paper bag with him. He reached into the paper bag and pulled out an entire army of firecrackers, all attached together. He put the firecracker armada down on the ground and proceeded to light the fuse. All of a sudden, all the firecrackers exploded. Burning firecracker embers wafted thru the air.

Sage did not move! She was the only horse not to move her feet. In fact, we had to dodge a burning ember.

"Sage the Brave" was firmly established!

MOUNTING A HORSE IS AN UPHILL BATTLE

The Level 1 clinic was three days long. It was July in Missouri. It was horrid hot and humid. I was doing fine, right along with everyone else. David told us that he was staying over on Monday, July 1st, and would do assessments on our Level 1 tasks. "Well, why not, I thought. Maybe I'll pass 4 tasks and just be that much ahead! No stress in this!"

We did the ground tasks and the last ground task was the mounting task. Here's the rule back then…Mount from the ground and no aid permitted… not a mounting block, stepstool, etc.. Nothing.

During my weekly lessons with Karen Moulis, she always had me try to mount. I always failed. She advised me to climb stairs, 2 or 3 steps at a time. I work in an 18 story building so I took to climbing stairs. I found the tractor at home makes a great mounting exercise. Because of the tractor steering wheel, I could actually pull myself up and down. I bought stirrups and straps. I was going to mount the stirrups to a fence and practice mounting. That didn't work at all.

I also attempted to lose weight. That was a good diet fear. Lose weight or not pass Level 1!

The time for the mounting task with David Lichman had arrived. Karen and Jenny huddled with me in the barn aisle for a pep talk session. "You can do it! You can do it! Know you can do it!" I sailed out of the huddle high on confidence and power to Sage, waiting for me in the arena. I pulled her back and forth so she would set her feet wide for the big "pull" moment. I put my foot in the stirrup and hopped around to get one hand in the mane and the other on the cantle. I was aware that this was "mount or die" day. I was charged by my pep talk. I felt like I could mount a mountain!

Hey Ha! I put forth a mountain of power and sailed right up in the stirrup. The rule is you stand in the stirrup with your hip into the saddle. That's exactly where I was, being the queen of mounting. This is the first time ever that I made it up in the saddle. I felt exaltation.

Let's go to Sage's point of view. This ponderous human had never put this much power into mounting. The heavy pull of my body surprised her. She had set her feet wide, but never experienced this wrenching sideways pull.

Sage lost her balance and began to stumble, trying to get her balance. I was standing in the saddle stirrup looking at David Lichman with triumph. I could see his face crumple into frown lines of concern. He said, "Get Off."

Here we are back with my point of view. "Get Off? What is he talking about? I'm in the saddle. I'm seconds away from swinging my leg over and sitting in the saddle. Get off? I've been trying to mount a horse for months and months and he wants me to get off now? No Way!"

Then Sage fell. She fell down to the ground with me standing in the stirrup like I was the captain of a sinking boat. Gravity being what it is, I fell to the ground. I rolled besides her and stayed. I was still excited that I had gotten up in the stirrup! I had mounted Sage, all except the part where you swing your leg over. Shoot, that was a given! I mounted Sage! I saw David's head leaning over me with an expression of deep concern. "Are you OK?"

I sat up and eagerly said, "Did I pass?"

David Lichman looked at me with the expression of "Are you crazy" and walked away. I didn't pass the mounting test on July 1st.

LEVEL ONE TASKS- JULY 1996

After the excitement of the failed mounting task, we took a lunch break. Sitting in the air conditioned lounge with my food, I started to cry.

What the heck? I wasn't unhappy. Fortunately I had a similar experience in my prior long distance biking hobby. I figured out that I was experiencing heat exhaustion. It was nearly 90 degrees and this was the fourth day I had been in this heat.

"Don't worry, I said to David and the surprised crowd of people getting assessed along with me. I'm just suffering a little bit from heat exhaustion. I'm not really crying."

Before I could say, "Boy Howdy!", I had a glass of water to drink and a couple of cold towels to rub on my face and arms. I recovered and went out to be assessed in the riding tasks.

LEVEL 1 TASKS – Passed Level 1 **1/24/1997** PNH Assessor: Jill Matthews "Congratulations on all your accomplishments

Task	My comments or further explanation of task
Approach your horse from 10' away. Rub horse from head to tail with Halter. Show you can clean all four feet from one side. Fit and correctly tie the Natural Halter	Horse is loose. Have you ever tried to pick up all four feet from one side of the horse? Try it!
Show the 7 Games on the ground • The Friendly Game • The Porcupine Game • The Driving Game • The Yo Yo Game • The Circling Game • The Sideways Game • The Squeeze Game	

Trailer load with friendly swing of 12' rope	Send the horse into the trailer and swing the rope over the back of the horse
Bareback mounting with help	Another human's thigh becomes your mounting block-that's how my friend got me on Sage at the Eminence water disaster.
Demonstrate Lateral flexion	Bend horse's head to left and right without her moving the feet
Ride Bareback with Parelli Natural Halter and Horseman String (six foot rope). Walk and Trot a full figure 8, then change string to the other side and repeat. Ride towards camera/Assessor and come down to a Halt and Back-Up	Failed-I couldn't get Sage to keep in the trot and do a figure 8. This involved neck reining or her following my body language and we were nowhere near ready for that.
Saddle from the Indian Side	Calvary manuals taught the entire human race stand on the left side of the horse and put the saddle on. Indian side is the right side. There's much advantage to putting a western saddle on the left side.
Mounting Task, both sides	Failed, sniffle
Ride with Parelli Natural Halter, Horseman's String & Carrot Stick. Show a Figure 8 at a trot	I got the figure 8 on this one, but could not keep her in a "trot" gait. failed
Bridle your horse from your knees and remove natural halter from under bridle	passed
Show Indirect Rein and Direct Rein. Demonstrate with turns to the left and then the right...Indirect, then Direct in a continuous flow	Turn a 360 doing first the indirect and then the direct. Horse's front legs should cross over from the front and then on the indirect, the back legs cross under the body.

Ride from the Halt up into a Walk, Trot and Canter on a loose rein	No problem!
Stop from the Canter Using one rein	One rein bend to a stop. We don't pull back on the reins to stop
Trotting Task (posting)	Sit the trot, post the trot, bounce with the trot and stand in the saddle at the trot. Yes, you can post with gaited horses. It is harder as you have no suspension to send your body "up".
Show turns at the Trot (half circle to the right & to the left)	Failed as we couldn't consistently keep in a "trotting" gait.
Trot a straight line toward the Camera / Assessor, come down to a Stop & Back-Up maintaining the Focus and Straightness	Focus is important. The horse has to go forward straight, stop straight and back straight
Sideways Task	Sidepass is both front and legs cross over and the horse goes sideways. We could use the arena wall or fence to help this out.
Controlled Catastrophe	We passed this during the clinic with the firecrackers!

At that time, tasks were passed with Excellence or Pass. Instructors had to pass all tasks "with Excellence".

Amazingly, I passed all but four tasks when I expected maybe I would pass four tasks. I was a happy and exhausted Parelli student after this clinic!

Thank you David Lichman for your many clinics and help to attaining my dream with horses.

In January 1997, I videotaped the remaining 4 tasks and got the word back by mail that I had passed. Later I got my Level 1 Certificate in the mail. Horse genes were smiling big on that grand day!

HORSE FOR A 48 YEAR OLD BEGINNING ADULT RIDER

- Been-there-done-that horse
- Has experienced much in the real world of shows, trail riding or going to events
- Desensitized to everything
- Doesn't explode straight up, sideways and/or bolt at strange objects, deer, turkey, mountain lions in bushes, bikes, kites, etc.
- Loads and unloads into and out of a trailer without fear
- On the scale of 1-10, be a 2 or 3 in willing to go forward.
- Missouri Fox Trotter

Green on green worked out for me. That's how I found Jennifer Vaught to train my horses. I had Karen Moulis and Jenny Vaught give me lessons. I had a nice safe confident lesson horse. I had the Parelli system which gave me baby step goals with safety being the main concern. Starting with a two-year-old gave me a lot of experience with dealing with fear. Without Jenny Vaught, my horse experience might have lasted two years or less and I would have joined the legion of people with horse genes, but too scared to ride.

Back in the 90s and early 2000 years, the Parelli's had not identified the different horse personality types. Luckily, Sage and Velvet were the best personality type for me, left brain introverts. I don't believe it matters what personality type I am, it matters that I keep my confidence. An introvert horse is less likely to move their feet forward than an extrovert horse. Left brain is a confident horse less likely to move forward in spurts of scary speed.

If I had taken my friend's advice and found the mythical 12-year-old-been-there-done-that gelding, my life would have been much different. I would have not suffered from all this fear. I probably would not understand horses. I wouldn't have bonded deeply with my horses. I wouldn't have had to overcome fear. I went through two deep fears with my first two horses. I went through another deep fear with another horse and that's another book to come. I wouldn't be able to read body language and sense what people are really like. Study this natural horsemanship stuff and you'll learn to read body language of both horses and humans!

SAGE – WILLFUL LEFT BRAIN INTROVERT

When I started riding Sage out in the real world, she became a dominant lead horse with argue. I was at home and rode Sage out of sight from Velvet. All of a sudden, Sage started rearing. That's what I thought it was at the moment. She was really having an argument with me about going away from Velvet. She hopped up and down with her front legs and refused to move forward. She was having an argue moment of "I don't want to go this way!" My brain told me she was rearing and wondered what to do about it. I became frightened and it took three hops before I was able to come up with the answer I had been taught. "Bend her!" Horses cannot rear when their head is bent around to your leg. I bent her head around and the rearing stopped. "Good Lord," I wondered why it had taken me so long to bend that head. My brain knew what to do, but my body didn't. It took a while for the brain to be able to convince the body to take the bending action. Brains can think stuff, but whey your body muscles are frozen, they can't obey the brain.

On another ride, we were farther away from home and Sage bucked. My brain froze in shock. Here's where we say a little prayer of thanks for gaited horses. Many of them have no or little suspension. When Sage bucked, she put her head down and kicked her back legs up. Sage bucked three times and I stayed on! There was no rodeo bucking horse leaping up into the air for my Sage. Again, it took my brain a long time to figure out what to do. Bend her! A horse can't buck when the head is bent around to your knee.

I lived through the bucking and immediately sought Jenny's advice. Her eyes narrowed which is a sign of agitation. This time it was poor Sage who would get the impact of that advice. My advice from Jenny, "She will do it again. When she does, get off and make her wish that you were on her back. Backing and sidepassing with effort is what you will ask of her." The "with effort" part of this advice is that they will need to move out!

As predicted, Sage bucked again. I dismounted. We sidepassed and backed very quickly for about thirty minutes. She also had to canter or gallop in a circle. When she got out of breath, we backed and then we sidepassed. When she carried her head down low, I got back on her and we sedately continued our trip away from home. That was a one bottle wine night.

This bucking and hopping is something that left brain introvert horses will do to argue.
If Sage had won, she would have done it more often. Every now and then, she would test out the bucking argument for a couple of years after that. Her hopping argument continues to this day on rare occasions when she is ridden too long or asked to go somewhere alone where she doesn't want to go!

On trail rides with a certain number of horses, Sage demanded to be the lead horse. I think I had it down to 6-7 horses to ride with when she started insisting on leading the herd. The insisting part consisted of wanting badly to pass the horse in front of her. She tries to go faster than the horse in front of her. She tries to speed up and pass. It was my job to slow her down. I used the one rein, slow down approach. Bend her head until she slowed down and then let the rein loose.

Our adventure with North American Trail Riding Competition showed off her willful dominant self beautifully. Firstly, there usually are way more than seven horses competing. We all gather at the start of the trail and are sent off individually or in small groups. On our first competition, Sage did not get to lead the ride. Horses took off and Sage was asked to stand and wait. She hated that! She started prancing around with occasional bucks. I got to bend her head around a whole bunch of times before we got to start. We headed out in our small group, but Sage was very insistent that she pass all the horses in our group and catch up with those leading horses. Oh my! It took me 30-45 minutes of constant bending to get her slowed down where she would just follow the horse in front of her. We sidepassed on the wider spots of the trail. Finally, she became capable of following the horses in our group. The second day that we rode, she was fine!

Long after this happened, we went on another trail ride with a bunch of horses. It was an organized ride and we had to do an obstacle at set points. While you do the obstacle, the horses in front of you leave. Even after many years of training, Sage reverted to her dominant lead horse. She could think of nothing than to catch up with the leading horses. The other horses went out of sight and we were at the bottom of a steep hill. We cantered sideways up the hill. How exciting was that! I figured letting her canter sideways in control was better than her throwing a fit and bucking when I tried to stop her forward motion! The person after me had a horse that wanted to race the wind and get with the herd also. She thanked me after I had cantered up the hill. Sage's body took up the entire width of the trail so her horse couldn't get around. Sage saved her from riding a bolting horse! "Oh pshaw," I said. "It was nothing." My blood pressure was probably about 500 or so, but I looked calm on the outside.

Our second North American Trail Ride Competition was where Sage learned a balking trick. We would be zipping along with the other horses. She signaled that she had to stop and urinate. She had to stop and do this more than the other horses in our group!

This particular trail ride had many hills. We are encouraged to stand up in the stirrups to get the weight off the horse's back when climbing a hill. We are judged on this. I didn't have the skill to do this. When Sage surged upwards in a canter, my body fell back down on the saddle. I didn't know that it was better to have her walk up these steep hills. She wanted to run up the hills. It was fun, so I let her do it.

After the trail ride was over and we were back at the trailer, she laid down. We checked her back and she was sore. My thumping down in the saddle made her sore. We didn't compete the second day. I never competed in another NATRC ride again. I remain a little grumpy about the standing up out of the saddle. The rides were all day Saturday and Sunday. You had to take off work to be there on the Friday. They have one-day rides now, but I never got back into it. I'm not an avid fan of long trail rides. I'm an avid fan of training and learning.

I took Sage home and rode her after she had recovered. She kept stopping and appeared to want to urinate. Sometimes after a while, she did urinate and sometimes, she never did. Not long after this, white spots appeared on her withers where the saddle had put too much pressure and killed the ability of the blood to run through her cells. I decided Sage had kidney damage and that explained why she was stopping so much. I took her to the vet to see about her kidney damage. "Hmmmm," the vet said. "There's a lot of muscle and tissue between where you sit and where the kidneys are. Surely no damage here."

I knew better. Sage was given about six months off to recover from kidney damage. Thankfully, I had the backup horse, Velvet, to ride!

SADDLE FIT

I bought Nikken round magnets and duck taped them to Sage's white spots on her withers. One magnet fell off after a few days, but the other stayed on. The white spot gradually disappeared as the circulation returned. I got intrigued with saddle fitting and expensive pads.

Here is the short version of what I discovered. Sage did not have kidney damage. It was a trick that she figured out to balk. Her wanting to stop to urinate is a successful balking maneuver. She fooled me for years! These left brained introvert horses are masters of the stop!

The venture I had into saddle fitting takes another book. I spent a lot of money to find the perfect saddle and saddle pad. I thought you could solve the problem of saddle fit with money. I found out that is not a true statement. I got saddles that fit her wide withers. I got ergonomic saddle pads. Sage had another problem which no one addressed back in the late 90's up to this very moment and into the far-ever future. Turns out Sage was slightly downhill. Her withers were lower than her back. The saddle was pushing downhill and landing on her withers. That was the cause of the pressure. I now own a CSI Saddle Pad. It has bullet proof Kevlar inside the padding. When a horse is downhill, the Kevlar material does not let pressure come through from the saddle to the horse! If it can stop a bullet, it can stop the pain of saddle pressure.

CLINIC FASHION WEAR ADVICE

Velvet started her training with Jenny early the next year after Sage had been started. I didn't have them both in training at the same time. When I had bad experiences with Sage, she returned to Jenny for more training. She was in training to be a "beginner's horse". Some of you have already experienced how difficult life can be when both you and your horse are beginners. We call that "green on green makes black and blue".

Sage is the go-to horse and Velvet became the secondary horse. Velvet had been in training long enough that I got those words again, "Velvet is ready for you to ride."

Unlike those same word experience when I first rode Sage, riding Velvet was a good experience. Velvet is a horse that tries, and she does not fiercely dominate. We clicked! At this time, Pine Dell Farm was scheduled to have a Parelli Natural Horsemanship Level 1 clinic with Neal Pye. I decided to ride Velvet in the clinic with Jenny's approval.

Natural Horsemanship was new to the Midwest. Clinics attracted 40-50 auditors and this was no exception. We had the crowd, and Neil Pye with his Australian accent!

The clinic started with Neal and the clinic participants. Each of us told Neal our name and what we were doing with our horse. I told Neal that I was riding a two-year-old and I had ridden her nine times. His eyebrows shot up! "Nine Rides?" he said. "Yes," I smiled in reply. This is where Jenny entered the conversation and told him that she had started Velvet, and Velvet and I were in training with her. She further stated that Velvet and I were doing well together. Neal's eyebrows came down to his normal eyebrow resting place and moved on to the next person. I ignored the eyebrows because Velvet and I were a confident team.

During this time of my life, I dressed like I was in a show ring instead of a clinic. I assume that people would watch my horse and me and be very impressed. The smart thing to do to ensure that they did watch me was to dress nicely. I had a disdain for people who wore plain old faded T shirts in these clinics. Here I had an audience of fifty people plus the instructor watching me. I dressed up! I even wore earrings!

Watch Me! Watch Me! It's a personality disorder that I have.

One of the tasks in Level 1, at that time, was Assisted Mounting. A person would stand by your horse with one hand hanging on to the horse's mane. The person would kneel with one leg. The rider would step up on the helper's kneeling thigh. The assistant person would then grab the rider's leg to provide stability and the rider used the assistant's thigh as a mounting block. The assistant did not need to lift the rider, just provide stability during the mount.

I was wearing my newest cowboy shirt. It was red, black and yellow. It had black horses running across the landscape outlined with red flame on a yellow background. It was a spectacular shirt. No one could look anywhere else but at my shirt.

I had a helper from the audience help me mount. He was a 5' 11" strong guy. When he grabbed my leg, he broke the rules. When I pushed off his thigh to mount, he also flung me upwards. I went up on my horse, over the other side and landed in a puddle of flaming black horses on a yellow background – in the dirt.

That is when I learned that it might be best not to draw attention to one's self. If I had had a plain T-shirt on, maybe 50 people would not have seen the spectacle ending with me Ker-splat on the ground. I leaped to my feet and quickly checked out the crowd to see if any of them were laughing.

When you see me riding in a clinic now, I will have a T shirt on. I try to have Missouri Fox Trotter T-shirt on or a T-shirt with horses on it. It usually is faded. I no longer want the crowd to zero in on me until I do a positive kind of showing off. Yep, I learned that lesson!

GROUP LESSONS – OBSESSED WITH LEARNING

I passed Level one and moved on to group lessons with Jenny Vaught. This is when my total obsession with learning started. My horse genes went out of control. I've never succeeded in reining them in. I had been taking one private lesson a week with Karen Moulis, Jenny's mother. Somewhere along the line, I discovered that Jenny gave group lessons. I discovered group lesson heaven! I moved to Jenny's lessons.

Jenny was a certified Parelli instructor and she traveled to Colorado to ride with Pat and Linda Parelli at least once a year. When she came back, the group lessons were her testing ground for all the new things she had learned with Pat and Linda. We loved it!

Jenny was giving one-hour lessons two nights a week and a two-hour lesson on Saturday morning. I took them all! I was getting four plus hours per week and my understanding of all things horse, accelerated.

After I graduated from Level 1, I took a look at the Level 2 Tasks. They were immense and complex. I didn't understand some of them. I thought most of them were impossible for me to accomplish. I read the tasks. I closed the pamphlet and put it away. I was content to head in the direction in which Jenny was pointing me. She took me steadily down the knowledge-with-horses path. There were some high points and some self-induced low points.

All the Parelli tasks have now changed. We don't even call them tasks anymore. It is a much easier progression through the horse learning journey.

Jenny's students are dedicated to her and their horse journey. My best friends, young and old, took part in the group lessons, every week, every month and every year. We progressed. We were always challenged to go beyond our comfort zone at least once per lesson. We didn't have an upper level temperature to cancel our lessons. In the winter if it was below 20 degrees, we cancelled! I fried and froze. I had wonderful fun and whined during the fried and frozen parts…just a little! After all these years, one person remains steady in most of the lessons that Jenny gives at Pine Dell Farm. She also was in the arena when I first rode Sage. Patty is on her second horse now. I'm on my 6th horse, with a mule having been thrown in along the journey!

I'll go on some more about Jenny. She is my life-long friend. She is true blue through and through. She is always interested in your point of view and always considers what you have said. If it were me after I've heard the same thing at least 1500 times, I would have stopped listening long ago. Jenny is not like that. She listens. She is sympathetic. She understands. She pushes her students towards excellence, step by baby step.

BATTLE OF THE EXTROVERT AND THE INTROVERT

I haven't talked much about Sage's personality. Sage is usually the dominant horse in any crowd. She is a left-brain introvert and very confident in herself. She argues. We call a horse like this "willful". I'm a left brain extrovert and used to getting my own way.

During our journey together, Sage and I had thousands of battles over who got to be the dominant mare. In the early years, Sage won most of the battles. We had a point system. On a day where she won, she might have been awarded 5000 points to my 5 points. Sage won because she was experienced in being a left-brain horse. I lost because of my inexperience and my fear. Whenever I went into right-brain fear, Sage was right there to lead me where she wanted to go!

Oh, I got the exercise all right! Sage made me very healthy! Whenever she went into the hopping or bucking mode, I got a lot of ground exercise. I was able to stay left-brain more and win more points over Sage.

We finally ended most of the bucking towards the end of our Level 2 journey. It got so she would take one or two fun bucks when she was cantering up a hill. Amazingly, I was able to ride those out and enjoy them. I just ignored her bucking and finally it went away!

SADDLE BUCKING

On an evening ride, I am dedicated to cantering and galloping on Sage. I will not tense up. I will allow my hands to be quiet. I will not pick up the reins and hold them up to my nose. I will not tense up my shoulders.

Sage is a well-trained horse. I decided to skip all my normal preflight check out. We walked up to the upper 40 acres. I tightened the girth several times and got on. The girth was tight.

We went out to the 40 acre flat field. I asked Sage to canter, and away we went. I was doing great. I was rocking in the saddle in time with her body. My knees were naturally bent. My hands were quiet and my shoulders relaxed.

All of sudden, Sage was bucking with me! I pulled up on her head, trying to stop the bucking. I became tight with tension. I thought evil thoughts about Sage. I got her stopped, but she kept bucking every few moments. I pulled her head up again. She stood stock-still. I leaned forward and Sage bucked.

How is Sage bucking when she is standing stone still?

No, it wasn't Sage. The saddle had slipped. I was riding her neck! When I leaned forward, the back of the saddle tipped up! Whoa! This is a precarious situation!

I decided that I needed to get off, RIGHT AWAY! I leaned forward, preparing to swing my leg over, and the back of the saddle bucked. I did that again, just to make certain. Yep. It bucked again.

OK, I'll ride very slowly and quietly to a mounting block. Walk walk....oh Wow! The saddle is just balanced on her neck. There's no round body to hold it in place. I have to get off before I fall off! Maybe I'll have to fall off to get off.

You know the alarm that starts in your toes and goes clear through your body till it gets to your brain? Finally, your brain says, "SCREAM!"

I looked around for a miracle. There was no miracle to help me. I tried to get my leg over the back of the saddle without bending forward. Do you know how hard that is? Finally, I got my leg on the back of the saddle which held it down enough so that I could get off.

I apologized to Sage for treating her so badly. She never did buck.

We walked back to the outside arena. I told someone about the saddle. He wanted to know "WHAT HAPPENED?" He was looking for dirt marks and blood. I told him the saddle tipped forward! He asked me if I was able to land on two feet. He was impressed when I told him that I was able to dismount and land on two feet. He quit looking for the blood.

After a good preflight checkout, I rode Sage again. We did canter again for a short distance. I imagined that my body motion was forcing the saddle to creep forward. Concern/fear won and I stopped cantering. From now on, we are going to canter and jump something on the ground...and tighten the girth at least 3 times before I get on. These are the rules, I broke them and the saddle tried to buck me off. Never again will I break the rules! Sage got many extra treats! Poor abused horse.

BUGGY LOVE

It was a work trip. My co-worker and I driving somewhere in northern Iowa. We stopped at an antique store and lo and behold, they had a Doctor's Buggy in the store. It was the most beautiful thing I had ever seen. Instantly, I was driving the buggy with my trusty beautiful horse Sage! I was transfixed. "How Much", said I. The answer was $affordable. I bought the buggy and told the owners that I would be back in a week to pick up the buggy and transfer it home to Missouri.

The very next day that I arrived home, I hired Jenny to teach Sage how to drive. Someone on the Internet horse advice world told me that horses need to be trained to pull a buggy. It was a safety thing. OK!

Jenny grimaced. She is not a driving person. "Only for you. Only because Sage has already been trained and understands what the bridle says. I don't like to hitch up young green horses to a buggy as their mouths have not yet been trained to understand the bit. For Sage, I will do it."

YAY! Thank You. Thank You.

A day later, I drove my horse trailer (no horse inside) over something that stuck underneath it. "Scream, Scrap", it yelled. The noise kept on. I drove truck and trailer into a big parking lot that had just the smallest of an incline. I decided to back the trailer to try to get rid of whatever that was screeching under the trailer.

Let's do a background story before going on with the story. New owner to truck and trailer took lessons from spouse on how to drive trailer. This is a short bed truck with a gooseneck hitch. I learned how nifty this gooseneck trailer is because you can back without it hitting the truck, no matter how crooked you back. Sadly, there was a piece of information missing from spouse trailer training.

Jackknife.

Unbelievable I backed the trailer just the slightest bit crooked up the slightest bit of a hill and the trailer came through the back window. The new word is Jackknife. Your horse trailer can break your truck window, especially since it is a short bed truck. My back truck window was broken!

I was due to drive to Iowa to get the buggy the very next day! My spouse and my mother went with me. It was just a little bit on the cold side and we had to turn on the heater full blast to be comfy. That's because there is a slight breeze from the back broken window.

No problem. We got the buggy. Somehow it was loaded on our flatbed trailer and home we went. We delivered the buggy to Pine Dell and I waited for my part of the training. I purchased a harness. What a confusing mess of stuff is a harness!

A while later I started taking driving lessons with Sage minus the buggy. I drove a tire around. Jenny had me drive a pole around. I had to learn how to negotiate a pulled thing around corners without mashing the fake buggy. I graduated to pulling the fake buggy around the road around Pine Dell.

A big day came and I was hitched up to a cart. I sat in and drove the cart around the arena and out into the outside world. I was able to get around without smashing anything.

I learned how to put my harness on Sage. I practiced. Sage became a buggy horse with Jenny's training. I became a buggy person with Jenny's training.

The next step was my buggy. Oh this is so sexy.

We hitched the buggy up at Pine Dell. Sage seemed to struggle a bit to walk off. Oh, the buggy is a lot heavier than the cart! Off we went around the Pine Dell roads. I discovered that a horse's tail is irritating when driving a buggy. When she swished at a fly, her tail got caught in the reins. How irritating was that.

I passed buggy driving 101 and Sage and I got to go home along with the buggy. It was a chilly pre-winter day. I got all my heavy clothes on and a warm hat. I came out into the world and hitched Sage up to the buggy. I am a harness expert.

I drove Sage out of the farm drive to the gravel road that leads to our house. I drove up the road. Going at a walk was pretty boring, so we went faster. Not long after that, we cantered. It seemed to be going all right. I wondered if buggy cantering was legal. Sage slowed down and we turned around in the same parking lot that crashed my back truck window months earlier. We headed back home. It was cold. It was boring. I just sat in the buggy and got colder. Driving Sage was darn easy. It was too easy.

I unhitched Sage and never drove again. Years later we sold the buggy before it fell apart. I am not a driving person. I am a rider! Sage is a trained buggy horse. No one in my world cares.

Pony Horse Problem

The term "pony horse" is used when you ride a horse and lead another horse. There are many reasons to "pony a horse". I had decided to go for a ride and exercise two horses at the same time. I rode Sage and led Velvet out into the great expanse of my neighbor's turf farm. Velvet started to rear and buck and run back and forth on the "pony side". I knew we had trouble in River City!

I had to concentrate on keeping my leg from being tangled up in the lead rope.
Velvet also rubbed and pushed against Sage, close to where my leg hangs down. Sage held firm. I lost all control of the lead rope. Velvet went behind Sage and up on the other side where she became snubbed. Her head was right above my knee and she could not move. At least that helped me be able to find the lead rope. It was under the saddle fender. The lead rope went around Sage's rear end. I managed to get the lead rope loose and threw it Velvet's way. Velvet took off galloping. She went right into the barn.

Sage and I trotted down to the barn. I got off and spied Velvet in the back portion of her stall. I tied Sage up and came back to the stall where I had to do battle with a huge bumblebee. It was waiting in attack mode. Thank goodness, I was carrying Sage's fly mask. The bumblebee and I did several dances in the aisle. Finally, he gave up and flew away. Sage got extra treats for staying calm and thus saving my life! Velvet got extra treats to make up for the stings. I had a wine bottle treat.

Did She fox Trot?

One weekend, my good friend, Ken Kemp, came to ride with me. He probably came for some other reason, like to attend a Parelli clinic or ride in the Kansas City Regional Fox Trotter horse show. But on this day, we were out riding at my favorite park, James A. Reed My horsemanship skills had much improved and I was starting to figure out how to get Sage to do something other than a pace. I had Ken ride behind Sage and tell me what gait we were doing. One moment, he called out "flat foot walk". I nearly fell off Sage in happiness.

Turns out with Sage, all I had to do when she paced was post. Something about my posting made her legs want to do a flat foot walk or a running walk. Ken helped me out that day, telling me what my horse was doing. A gaited horse can be doing a different gait every two to three steps. Just when your body figures out what might be happening to those gaited legs, they switch to another gait. Here's the choices we have: dog walk, flat foot walk, pace, running walk, fox trot, rack, stepping pace, hard trot, fox walk, pace walk. The list goes on and on. Your body has to feel what the feet are doing. This is one of the reasons why gaited horses are master class. You need to "feel" what the horse's feet are doing and decide what is happening. If the gait is something you don't want, you have to fix it immediately.

Ken is a master at determining the horse's gaits. I went on a weekend trail ride with him once and he had just got the new tape, Gaits of the Missouri Fox Trotter. We watched the tape in his trailer living quarters three times in a row. Ken was in total rapt attention every second of the video. I lost my attentiveness after the second time. I bet Ken has watched that tape a few more times since then.

Ken and I were out that same weekend riding the trails. He was riding Silver, a tall Missouri Fox Trotter. Ken and his horse were riding in front of me and came to a tree with sturdy low branches. He thought he could duck and get under the tree. Ken was wrong. When he determined that the tree branch was going to win, he grabbed the branch in a bear hug. His horse went on and left Ken dangling on the branch. If that had been me, I would have just let myself be knocked off the horse by the branch. I would have never thought to grab the branch. His horse stopped and wondered where his rider had gone. Never had Silver been dismounted like that! Ken lowered himself from the tree, dropped to the ground, got back on his horse and we rode off.

November Swim-Ride

Back in the early years of Velvet and me is the story of the back property trail ride. Oh my goodness.

My new best friend, Lanie, brought her horse, Sparkles, and her husband, Tim, over to the house. Husbands went to the shop. Equestrians got on their horses. We were exploring my 29 1/2 acres of forest, creek, glen and glade. We explored the neighbor's acres too. Oh, what a marvelous time were Lanie and I having on our horses, Sparkles and Velvet.

We came upon Big Creek running through the back property. We came down a slight hill to the creek. It was shallow and we could walk right into it. We decided the stream was an easy way to get back to my property instead of returning through the forest path. We trail riders never like having to retrace the route. We forge ahead and blaze new trails and have new experiences. Boy Howdy!

We were walking through the stream. Both Lanie and I were feeling right proud of ourselves. We were being brave enough to ask our horses to walk in the stream and having them say YES MAM! We came to a deeper place in the stream. Velvet was walking in water above her ankles.

Suddenly, Velvet, my co-pilot, decided to leap out of the stream up on the bank. She did not check in with the pilot (me). Sparkles decided leaping out of the stream was a good idea too. Sparkles leaped up and landed right beside Velvet on the bank of the creek.

Lanie and I were both still in the saddle. That was surprising and very nice. It didn't last long. Velvet and Sparkles tried to move. They tried to walk up the side of the bank. Sadly, they were stuck. No moving because their legs had sunk into deep mud...right up to their knees.

Velvet and Sparkles thrashed without anything happening. They were struggling to get their legs out of the mud. Lanie and I were still sitting in the saddle wondering, "What is going to happen?"

Velvet decided to give a huge lunge upwards. She reared up with a ton and a half of power. She got free of the mud. She got free of me too. The law of physics dictated that my body fly into the air backwards. I was propelled thru the air and did the Apollo spacecraft splash-down in the deep part of the stream, right behind Velvet. I submerged! My head went under water!

While I was under the water, I worried that Velvet might come over backwards and crush me. We probably wouldn't have any more stories in this book if that would have happened! Thank God, Velvet stayed on her feet and clamored out of the mud.

Oh, I forgot to mention that this day was a chilly 40 degree fall day and I was wet from head to boots.

I managed to fly out of the water to the bank. Sparkles had lost her balance and fell over sideways on Lanie's leg. Sparkles, free of the mud, got up without stepping on Lanie. I watched it happen. It was slow motion horror.

Lanie was lying on the ground looking like she was alive, "Are you all right?!" I asked. She replied, "HELL NO"!

Turns out Lanie had a car accident earlier in her life and this was the bad leg from the car wreck. She had a titanium knee and this was the leg that was crushed by 1200 lbs. of horse. Sparkles isn't a thin horse.

Lanie dragged herself up and over to a tree. She clung there for a while telling me about her titanium knee between clenched teeth moans.

Then Lanie got on Sparkles. I got on Velvet. Yes, we were tough.

Probably a total of 30 minutes had gone by since we left our lovely husbands playing in the shop.

Here come the wives, wet and hurting. Both husbands' faces went from man cave happiness to horror. Both their jaws gaped and mouths opened as they beheld their wet, muddy wives and Lanie's obvious painful expression.

"What do you do with horses?" "I'm just a trail rider!" When you hear someone say, "I'm just a trail rider," smack them a good one. Trail riding can go from fun to disaster in a blink of an eyelash. "Just trail riding" is a dangerous sport.

Lanie died from lung cancer some years later and she is missed every day. RIP, Lanie.

So Old to Show

"Showtime", I thought as I lurched out of bed and listened to the rain. I thought about the mud on those two glistening horse hair bodies after yesterday's full body makeovers, nails done, expensive hairdos. I'm talking baths, scrubbing, rubbing, drying, clipping, sheening, and attempted braiding of manes and tails. Both Velvet and Sage were lovely; I was broken, old, sore-footed, wet, dirty and hairy. This is my first show as an adult. My last horse show was 33 years ago. I'm 50 years old and showing in my first horse show as an adult.

The rain had stopped. I went out to pasture and the horses were barely wet without any mud. Whew! Thank you up above! After breakfast, my husband's friend came over to play manly machine stuff. I was nervous about getting those fox trotter ribbons in Sage's and Velvet's mane and forelock. I asked John, who is a team roper, if he could braid my horse's hair. AHAHHHAAAA! John and my husband broke up over that. Braiding is not a manly team-roping thing. As they were spitting up with laughter, I promptly broke into sobbing sobs. All three of us were shocked! "Hmmm, we all thought, Susan is hysterical! Let's do calming words and thoughts and get her out of here!"

I got the horses into the trailer and drove the 10 miles, alternating with tears and deep breathing. What causes a calm, relaxed, don't-worry-till-it-happens person to experience such frightful feelings? This show stuff is hanging yourself out, with no defense, for strangers to judge in an arena where you are so inferior that you have to reach up to lick people's toes. It's way out of my comfort zone! I was totally in charge with the work part of my life. This horse show stuff is totally not-in-charge.

The week before the show, I was hysterical because I had never touched clippers and last braided anything 33 years ago. I did not want my horses pitied because I did not know how to make their fuzzy winter bodies into sleek summer splendor. Thank goodness, a friend volunteered to help so "my girls" were truly beautiful!

This is the 2nd annual horse show and seminar that the club has put on – purely for my benefit. The seminar teaches us about bits, training, and gaits. The horse show is for riders new to showing to get experience before we get thrown out with the wolves. This show is also for our experienced riders to get started in the current show year. Moreover, the experienced riders help us "newbies". This year the association president, Tom Owens, was the speaker and judge. I laughed at all his jokes, but it did not do any good in the show ring. Drat. He judged the horses on their performance rather than who laughed the most at his jokes.

My first hint of something going wrong was when the registration person said, "
Eight Classes? You want to sign up for eight classes?" I looked on the show bill again and counted. Yep, there were eight classes for me to ride in with Sage and Velvet. It was also then that I discovered that the show started at 1:30 rather than 2:00. I barely had time to saddle both horses, stab their ribbons on and get into the arena to warm up Sage for the trail class. I was at the trailer stabbing the ribbon into Sage's mane when another rider asked if the trail class allowed you to wear ribbons. Whoops! I looked at the rules and saw that it said, "No Ribbons"! I frantically sawed the ribbons out of Sage's mane and arrived at the gate. The frantic gate man was thrilled to find me. My number had been called several times. I was the next to last horse to perform in the trail class.

Sage, the fun events horse, has turned into the bravest horse ever. She was a formidable competitor with her trick bag of sidepassing, backing and tight fore and hindquarter turns. We had a blue tarp in the trail class and she just sailed over that. She sniggered at walking over the logs – come on give me a challenge! She sidepassed to the mailbox and waited patiently for me to get my letter in and out. She floated between two staked flags. "Is this the best you can do?" she asked in our first show ring experience.

When I came out, I leaped off Sage and traded her for Velvet, my "show horse". The next class was starting and Velvet's newly borrowed show bridle hung from the saddle horn instead of her head where I had put it. My husband had arrived to take care of my horses for me. He said, "Velvet hates her bit. Her borrowed bridle is too long and I can't control her!" Husband is also new to horses, and Velvet had gone hysterical when I took Sage away.

I was trying to get the bridle on Velvet, the hysterical horse, when the trail class riders and horses were called back into the arena to line up! HUH! Sage and my husband had disappeared. I had a hysterical Velvet on my hands. The brave gatekeeper volunteered to hold Velvet so I could return into the arena.

Susan, the new show horse person, cantered into the arena. I hoped people wouldn't notice that I wasn't riding a horse. There was a pregnant silence. They did notice. No one knew me then. They didn't know what an amazing humor I have. They thought I was a lunatic. The announcer was finally able to recover and made a quip about a funny lookin' two-legged horse in the arena. I lined up in the middle with the other horses and hoped my number would be called. It was! I got reserve! To thunderous applause, I cantered over to the ribbon girl and got my red beauty ribbon! I cantered out. Thank goodness I didn't win first or I would have had to canter a victory lap. Whew!!!

I scratched the bridleless horse from her first class and went out to do some calming groundwork. I hoped I might be able to get the bridle on before Velvet's next class! The classes that Sage and Velvet were in, alternated and the trailer was parked blocks away. I had planned to have different outfits for the fun events and the fox trotting events, but that wasn't going to work. I compromised with jeans and shiny silky jacket.

I lost the egg and spoon class when I believed the announcer who jokingly said, CANTER. That lost me the egg. No one else cantered.

We had a water relay where two riders had to work together. One had to dip water out of a bucket with plastic glass and then pour the water in the partner's plastic glass who then had to empty his glass' contents in the bucket. Then we had to bring the bucket to the judge's helper. We won!

We had musical feed sacks. When the music stopped, a horse had to get one foot on a feed bag. There was one less bag than horse in the arena. Sage was yelled at, threatened with ramming, but managed to STOMP on her sack. "Don't try messing with the boss Mare!" We lost when we were too far from a feed sack when the music stopped. The other horses beat us and were standing on the feed sack when we got there. I told Sage that we weren't allowed to knock a horse off the feed sack. We left the arena.

The husband loved Sage that day. He held her ribbons. He wore them on his overalls and stuck out his chest more as the day went by. Sage became "his horse" on this day.

Husband went up to the announcer and told him it was my first show. He did this while I was in the arena waiting for the next class to start. Husband also mentioned that I had young horses. I bet the announcer was just amazed to learn all this, but he dutifully reported it to the crowd. So, I had to ride around the arena. I waved at everyone with a big grin on my face and the Queen Elizabeth wave. Thank goodness, I was riding calm Sage. I told Sage to canter, but she wanted to pace instead. The crowd was nice to me and clapped.

Velvet, the former "sweet" horse now turned "spirited", electrified the crowd with her beauty and fire. Our performance at the gaits is not to be discussed. We did move quickly around the arena when asked to go into the fox trot. We just might have been hard trotting and not fox trotting. It appears that Velvet and I must get out more into the real world.

When the show mercifully ended, I was so grateful to Ronald Howe, the wonderful gate man who helped me get on my horse, held the classes open until I could get into the arena and tried to calm me down. My thanks to Ralph and Sue McGarry who gave me advice and also helped calm me down before entering the arena. Thanks to Paula Crump who gave me some training tips after the show was over, even though she worked harder than all the show horses and was dead tired. Thanks to Nancy McConnell who loaned me the show bridle. Thanks to Gail who fed me and wasn't afraid to hold the spirited Velvet. Thanks to all who helped a beginning adult rider survive her first show.

Thanks to my spouse. Lordy, what a day.

Sage and Susan are Fox Hunters

Fox hunters wear funny looking coats and those weird pants with long black boots. They ride with the hounds and chase a fox while seated on top of a patch of leather called an English saddle. This was not for me, living in Missouri where we pride ourselves on our Ozarks country ways.

My version of a fox hunter from the Ozarks was as follows: I've got my genuine pop gun toy rifle and wearing my coon skin cap. I've got my hounds tied to me, like field trial dogs, except my dogs are all stuffed doggies. They are tied to every place on the saddle that I can find, including one hanging from the bottom of the cinch, underneath Sage. When we zip along, the doggies bounce. I've got an antique fox head stole that I found in a clothing antique store. Sage is hidden under the fox pelt, so we can sneak up on brother fox. This is foxhunting at its finest.

My knee-high boots are John Deere bright green. I'm wearing antique black and red checkered wool winter hunting pants. I look amazing!

The fox head kept coming unattached from the fox pelt, so I had to carry the head in one hand. When I was in my two-handed cocking and shooting the rifle phase, I stuffed the head it in the saddle horn hole.

I was in a costume class rather than out in the Ozark wilderness chasing after brother fox.

Campout Sleeping Problems

My friends and I are the only tent people in the whole Ponderosa trail ride campground. It's 90+ and humid in the afternoon. The people with air-conditioned rigs head for air- conditioned naps after our noon meal. My two traveling companions with their bumper pull trailer drag their chairs to a tiny little two-year-old tree. Thy hover underneath the "not-wide" canopy of shade and try to nap.

Not me. I drag my extra special Wal-Mart air mattress...with the flocked top...out of my tent. I place it under the space between the back of the pickup and the gooseneck. I don't like to disconnect the trailer from the truck. Backing is involved to get it hitched up again. I loathe backing. The truck has a regular trailer hitch sticking out. I don't fit underneath that with the air mattress. The sun is shining straight down, no shade peeking on the side of anything. I wedge myself in the spot and take a nice little nap. I had only a few scrapes from banging into the annoying hitch. I felt special and rested with my wondrous flocked air mattress.

Three o'clock comes and the heat abated enough to make me want to get one of the horses out of the stall and do something. I kick the air mattress securely under the trailer and go get Sage. I tie her to the side of the trailer and proceed to clean out her stall. After a while, I knew I should check to see whether or not she had tangled her rope.

There was Sage ,in no trouble with the lead rope, but her two front feet were standing right in the middle of my air mattress! Scream! She had dug the air mattress out from underneath the trailer and was standing on it, on the flocked part!

I ran over and moved her feet off my precious air mattress. I took it over to a nice grassy place and flopped down on it. It was just fine, inflated and comfy. Whew! What a miracle to have my precious air mattress still alive.

Horse life went on in the campground and we had our evening trail ride. After dark, we sat outside and chatted until it was time to for me to hit the air mattress.

I crawled into my one-woman tent, getting all my stuff organized. Where's the flashlight? Where's the book? I'm settled down reading when I noticed that I was no longer supported by air. It was around 11:00, and I am lying on the hard ground. Oh groan wretched hardness of the real ground is agony. I moan. I tried to sleep on my pillows, but that's a poor excuse for a mattress. I gave that up about 2:00am. I slithered out of my tent and went to the pickup. My plan is to sleep in the front seat. I was being exceptionally quiet while throwing everything from the front seat to the back seat. A yell split the 2:am air. My husband yelled. He is sleeping in the gooseneck part of the trailer. I might have been quiet, but my actions broadcast as movement through the truck to the trailer hitch to the trailer. The husband woke up because his bedroom was shaking. The trailer had small, slit-like windows, so he was unable to peek out and see what was happening. He yelled, *"Just what do you think you're doing there!!!"*

I was shocked that he would talk to me in such a loud voice at that hour of the morning, so I went *shhhhhhh*! He is hard of hearing and did not hear the *shhhh*. He yelled the same words again at 2:02am in a campground! I ran back, opened the trailer door and told him once again to *shhhhh*! The next morning at breakfast, he was telling everyone that he thought someone was stealing the pickup. Since he was hitched up to the pickup, it made him just a little nervous to be clothing-less (naked), socked away in the trailer!

What a great night's sleep all the campers missed out on that night.

PAGOSA SPRINGS-PARELLI HEAVEN

The Mecca of the Parelli world is Pagosa Springs, Parelli Natural Horsemanship headquarters. Seekers of natural horsemanship from all over the world come to Pagosa Springs to learn from the best.

That is what Sage and I did! We went with my best friend, Lanie and her husband and her husband's brother. Our caravan was truck, trailer and car. We brought the car as a backup if the trailer broke down. We figured the car could go after help. Fortunately, since we had the car backup, the truck made it all the way to Pagosa Springs. It is about a 15-hour trip. I had to drive up and down Wolfe Creek Pass Mountain. That puts hair on your chest! Oh, shudder for that adventure. We took two days to get there. After Lanie and I were securely deposited at Parelli heaven, the two brothers went on a weeklong Colorado adventure with the car.

Lanie and I had signed up for Level 2 clinic. There were many instructors at the headquarters. No one was told who our instructor was going to be. Lanie and I knew Lee Smith from clinics at Pine Dell Farm. We prayed that we would get her to be our clinician. When we arrived, we were told that our clinician would be either Lee Smith or Linda Parelli. Our first day there, we saw Linda Parelli walking around. She was wearing breeches. She was thin and blond. No one I knew wore breeches in my world. Breeches are meant to be skin tight and reveal the body. I was horrified. I am a jeans girl. Since I am a curvy girl, I loved the rumpled look that hides fat. I tried not to stare, but it was difficult. Lanie and I prayed that we would get Lee Smith. I assumed Pat Parelli married Linda Parelli because she was thin and blond, not for her horsemanship or human communication skills!

Pat Parelli says, "When you make assumption, you make as "a**" of yourself." I'm glad I only shared that thought with Lanie! My assumption was way wrong. I found that out almost immediately when Linda took over our group.

We were immersed in a wonderful learning environment with Linda right from the beginning. Pat Parelli talked to us after dinner on the first night. We had guitar singing sessions. We had video submissions from students. We were told the story of Silke Valentine from East Germany. She is a paraplegic and has a Friesian horse. Her horse disrespected her so much that he stepped on and broke her feet. Being paraplegic, she couldn't feel anything when he broke her feet. She discovered her broken feet that night when she took off her boots. Silke started with the Parelli program and things changed with her and her horse. Pat went to visit with her when traveling in Europe. He was so impressed with her natural ability with horses that he paid for her and her horse to come to the USA and study with him! We got to see Silke's video audition for Level 1. She did things with her horse in the Level 1 video that I will never be able to do with my horses! I met Silke years later at Equitana.

We also had a couple of afternoon riding sessions with Pat Parelli. Three memories stand out from that week. One was the flying lead change logs. Many logs are laid end to end in a long meadow. We had to serpentine through the logs and try for a flying lead change every time we jumped the log. Yep, Sage and I must have jumped the logs about 50 times in one afternoon. I probably got some flying lead changes too, maybe one or two. The cantering and jumping memory will never go away. At least the logs were shorter than the barrels that Jenny always had me jump over at home!

The next memory is a simulation. We humans got a partner and simulated one being a human and the other one being a horse. We couldn't talk to our "horse". We had to play the 7 Games without talking. I decided to be a willful horse and not move when asked. Every other horse was polite with his or her human. That was just too easy for my human, who was a complete stranger to me. He asked me to do something and I refused. If I did move, it was as slow as molasses. I also leered at my human with my body language. "You can't make me" is what I was saying.

When a student is having trouble with a difficult horse, it is time for the instructor to help. Linda Parelli came into the round pen and took me on. She asked me to move. I refused. She asked at a phase 1. She asked me to move with a higher intensity and shook that carrot stick at me. That was a phase 2. I leered at her. Finally, after getting a firm intense look about her and shaking that stick faster (phase 3), she approached closer and closer. I was a bit nervous at her body energy, but stood my ground. She slapped my calf with the carrot stick and it stung. OUCH! That is called a phase 4. I leaped out of the way. She relaxed and rewarded me with a smile. Hmmm, I thought. Linda prepared to ask me to move again. Again, I did not believe her, and again, I was slapped with the carrot stick. Hey, it does not take me three times to learn. The third time she asked me to move, I was a willing horse. My attitude had made a big change. That lesson was a huge learning experience for me. Start at phase 1 and be willing to back it up with a phase 4. Be fair about it. When I encounter a stubborn horse, I try to follow the example that Linda Parelli personally demonstrated!

We got to watch Linda Parelli play with her own horse. We got to watch Pat have lesson with all the instructors that were there. We met all the instructors. Lanie and I graduated. We did well. I bet Jenny got many brownie points because Lanie and I were fabulous students!

1998 Missouri World Celebration Saturday

I decided to spend some special time with Velvet and see what the Missouri World Celebration Fox Trotter Horse Show is like. We arrived on Friday and found a place to park. I rode Velvet around on the grounds and had a great time. I took her back to the trailer and left her for about an hour while I shopped. It made me nervous to leave her alone any longer than an hour.

Velvet and I spent some of our time watching the horse show classes. I tried to stand where as many people as possible would see us. I found a triangle patch of grass right in the middle of a busy area on the show grounds. We hung out there hoping people would see us. I was brave back then. I had her bareback pad on her and was riding her with a Cherokee bridle. This was the six foot rope with loop in her mouth. That was her bit. I imagine people tried to avoid anyone looking like I did. Hundreds of people probably thought I was an alien. Several people did come over to meet us, and that was fun. When it was bedtime for Velvet and me, we hunted up a nice patch of ground in a lower area of the large show grounds. I heard my name called on the loud speaker, but it was much too late for me to get out of my tent, saddle up Velvet and appear anywhere.

Velvet and I spent an uncomfortable Friday night in the reedy lower pasture. I was in my tent with a punctured air mattress. Velvet pawed her reedy ground to make it comfy. Oh, we suffered.

Finally, 6:00am Saturday morning came, and we are up. At 7:00 am, I am to meet people who are interested in getting some information. They want names and addresses of people with nice trail riding fox trotters for sale. They want to find a duplicate Velvet at her breeder, Robert Lewis of Butler. They were intrigued about Natural Horsemanship training methods.

Velvet and I take care of our morning body, skin and hair care functions, adorn ourselves with makeup, and approve ourselves in the mirror. Of course, Velvet had her breakfast immediately upon my crawling out of the tent. I look for my purse. I look for my purse again. I look again, for my purse. The sudden glow of understanding lights up my brain. It wasn't one of my Internet boyfriends (Jeff, John, Craig…too many too list) trying to find me on the pager last night!. It was someone who had found my purse, paging me! A forgetful person who has lost my purse on many occasions, I expect my purse to be returned. I'll just check in at the office. Surely, with my luck, the purse will be there. I truly am Ms. Lucky!

I ask Velvet, "Please crawl into the trailer. We'll go up and find some nice grass." She complies. We start up the steep hill. Hmmm, the flint stone rocky road appears to be wet. Funny, it's in the middle of a drought, and the only wet stuff in sight is running down the road.

We charge up the very steep hill while water is coming down the road in a torrent. The truck starts slipping and the great adverse-condition driver (me) quickly slips into 4 wheel drive. Forward progress resumes. The road goes straight up. The water comes straight down. We slow and stall. Not being a stranger to being stuck in snow and ice (I'm originally from Iowa), I rock, turn the wheels, and rock. We rock great, but with zero movement. There is a semi-truck water storage unit, used to water the roads during the Celebration. Water is pouring out of the truck in a torrent at 6:45 am, right down our road. My tires are half buried in mud and I've made some dandy deep ruts. I am a woman alone, stuck with horse-in-trailer. It is 6:45am and I have to be at the cook shack in 15 minutes. I do what any red-blooded 50-year-old woman would do: I look desperately around for a male savior. Unfortunately, it's too early. All the male heroes are still asleep in their trailers. The thought occurred to me that Velvet weighs near 1000 lbs. I open the trailer door and tell the heavyweight to exit the trailer and go tie herself up. With a much lighter load, I pray that the truck will free itself. It does! It pops right out of the road rut and slowly tops the hill. Velvet whinnies in major relief. I cross myself.

I quickly find a nice grassy place to park and Velvet is tied where she can eat nice juicy grass. I quickly hike to the cook shack…penniless. The women are there and I lie and tell them that I don't eat breakfast. I "allow" them to buy me coffee. One of them brings her own buttered toast and offers me a piece. I don't let on that this piece of toast is all that is between me and death by breakfast-starvation.

After we are done talking, I hurriedly visit the office to ask about my purse. "NO PURSE has been turned in", the office woman says. I tell her that someone tried to page me last night from the cook shack. "It's probably still there, she said. "Grrrr." thought my tummy, "I could have had my purse and eaten breakfast,". I turn around to leave and in walks a man holding my purse. It was left in the cook shack overnight, and they decided that it was time to turn it into the office. See what I mean about my purse-return-luck?

Unfortunately, the purse was missing my cash. However, my credit cards and checkbook are intact. I am grateful to get the purse back with the important things. However, I still am penniless!

I walk hurriedly back and explained this money thing to Velvet. I promise her a nice surprise if she goes along with me. She agreed, knowing that her "momma gotta have money". She leaps into the trailer and off we go.

Guess what happens to the grounds on Saturday—the big night! Everyone starts coming into the grounds and parks with little car parts hanging out into the small road. The golf cart guy had to find the woman who stuck her bumper into the road, before I could get out. I had my own traffic jam! Finally, we made it to the highway and went into Ava. Thank goodness, a bank with an ATM exists on a big corner with plenty of turn around room. I don't mind backing when I'm all alone at my own property, but other people get mean when I take ½ hour to back 5 feet. I got money! We zipped across the road to McDonald's and finally got my breakfast. Whew.

With a lovely breakfast in hand, we zoomed out on the open road. Velvet wondered if I had lost my mind when we passed the Celebration grounds. Velvet's surprise breakfast was at the beautiful roadside park down the road from the Celebration grounds. She ate grass in the park and drank out of the babbling brook. I relaxed, knowing I had money and was again a citizen of the world.

We returned to the grounds and managed to squeeze the rig into a place where Velvet had room to stand and eat grass. I saddled up Velvet and off we went on a show ground tour. We discovered the back of the grounds and a narrow gravel flint road. Off we went down the pretty road. We were having a fine time looking at Ozark scenery when we heard hoof beats behind us. Shortly the hoof beats caught up with us and behold, a woman riding another beautiful black horse asked if she could ride with us! I found out that the black horse's breeding was the same as Velvet's, Toddy's Perfection. We chatted up a storm and she took me far down the road. We came out on the side of the highway north of the Celebration grounds. What a great ride it was, too. I have forgotten her name now. I hope she reads this. She invited Velvet and me to participate in the flag ceremony. I found out that she carried the Missouri flag!

As promised, we participated in the flag ceremony. Velvet has never carried a flag in her life, and it was windy. I was worried. Oh laugh at that! Flapping flag was no problem for Velvet. We got our flag. We got used to it. I let it go and it flapped over her head. Both of us disappeared inside the flag. She didn't move. The flag role call was called and away we went into the ring. What a thrill that was. I couldn't have wiped the grin off my face. We tried to go as wide as we could around the arena to make the time last longer. Another surprise was the announcing of both our names. We revel in the spotlight! The National Anthem was played and we all let the flags wave in the wind. Velvet and I choked up with the glory of it all.

For a lowly nobody…our names were announced over the loud speaker twice in our two days at AVA!

After the flag ceremony, I stood around and let people admire the beautiful Princess of the Pasture. Like any member of royalty, she could only take so much. She wanted to go back to the trailer and eat hay and grass. I enjoyed the rest of the Saturday night stake show! Of course, I had to check on her about every hour. It's an amazing amount of walking. Now everyone has golf carts to get around the show grounds.

That was the end of Ava adventure. When we awoke Sunday morning, the Celebration rain was hitting the ground. Taking down the tent in the rain was such a thrill. We drove home. I slept for 14 hours straight in my own lovely bed.

VELVET AND I IN A REINING CLASS.

Cow Pony Day One in November 1998

The Cow Clinic was out on 60 acres of land divided into three pastures. A herd of unlucky cows were minding their own business when 22 riders showed up.

It was the best clinic that I'd ever seen or participated in. It was 3 days of constant challenge. The 1st two days, we played games and were given tasks to increase the skills needed for working with cows. We played ground games with our horses to get them better at backing and "loading the hindquarters" so we could begin to get that "cutting horse" spin!. It was a Parelli Cow Clinic with David Ellis. Dave was in charge of our lives for 3 days from (9:00 am till dark thirty at 6:00pm)

Our "Ten-Commandment Unbreakable Cow Rule" was handed down from the instructor: "When the cow stops and turns, the horse and rider must back, make a small turn with the hindquarters followed by a "cutting horse" forequarter turn." If the cow beat us before we were able to get through the backing and hindquarter turn, we had to continue our maneuver, and then run fast to catch up with the cow.

On the horse, we were given an imaginary cow on our left or right to follow. Our cow turned, stopped, turned the other way and we had to focus on our imaginary cow. We had to follow the rules when the cow turned. Our imaginary cow waited for us while our horse followed the unbreakable cow rules.

Next, the horses and riders played follow the leader —nose to tail. We walked trotted and galloped to keep up with that tail in front of us.

Our instructor became the cow. We lined up side by side with our stirrups nearly touching. He was in the middle of our Calvary charge line and held up a stick so we all could see. Our task was to keep even with the "cow". He went forward, circled, went one way and then went another way. The RULE was hard to follow, and the cow faked us out a lot. The cow turned and the horses and riders did our backup, hindquarter and forequarter turn. By the time we were done with that, the cow had turned back the original direction and was way ahead of us…and this was at both the walk and then the trot. The cow turned and yelled, "GOTCHA!!!" We learned to back when the cow did a 180 until we were certain that the little bugger was going to stay in that direction. Then we did our quick back, turn, turn and run to catch up.

Synchronized Cow Riding didn't happen that day. We did get better. We all got better every day.

The riders circled the "Dave-pretend-cow" and stood pointed into the circle looking at the cow. The "pretend cow" tried to get out between the horses. The "cow" would stare at the hole, point at the hole and try to go through it. It was a very polite "cow" to tell us where he was going to try to escape. The riders were to back, turn the hindquarters, then the fore quarters and run to meet the neighbor horse nose to nose before the cow could get to the hole. The horses were to form a "gate" to block the cow from getting to the outside of the circle. Sage let the "cow" get through her gate plenty of times. Her problem was not the turns; it was the rushing to meet the nose of the other horse. Sage had no thought of rushing anywhere when my "cheeks" smiled and my legs squeezed. My "former" friend made disparaging remarks about detecting a "Sage slowness trend".

Sigh...

We learned the "outrider run." The "cow" took off straight towards the opposite corner of the large pasture. Two riders on each side galloped off at a 45-degree angle away from the cow. This maneuver fooled the "cow" into thinking we weren't chasing it. (It is forbidden to run all the valuable meat off the cow's body.) When the outriders get in front of the cow, they cut in and stop the cow. The two outriders are supposed to go the same speed and cut in front of the cow at the same time. Sage wasn't interested in going with impulsion to match the other rider.

Sage, the impulse-less, bucked when I gave her my body signs to gallop. She finally managed a slow canter, at first trying to run into the line of horses waiting their turn to be the outrider. She was telling everyone that she didn't want to leave the herd! We cantered slowly on her 1st outrun while our opposite rider knitted an entire sweater, waiting for us. After more outruns, Sage managed a slow gallop as her very fastest speed.

Thank you horse genes, Missouri Fox Trotter and the Parelli method for an impulse-less safe horse to ride, no matter that it gets frustrating.

COW PONY – DAY TWO

Working with real cows was much better than our pretend cow, clinician Dave Ellis. The real cow didn't yell at us about forgetting to back and to make a hindquarter turn when we got excited about keeping up with the cow. The real cow didn't yell at us at all! Instead, the real cow spurted around us and took off where ever it wanted to go. Real cows are merciless. They don't care about your feelings or desires. If they want to run past you, they usually do it. Real cows humiliate even experienced cowboys!

Our first task was to follow the same cow around for about 15 minutes to give the horse an idea that we were focused on a cow. "What fun!" Sage thought; "Let's play with cows every day." She enjoyed her time in following one cow, but she didn't catch on to the idea that it was her cow.

We spent Saturday and Sunday herding and driving cows in many ways:

Driving with many riders in a "U" shape.

Driving with few riders in a "U" shape

Driving with horses nose to tail. This meant that one horse did the driving and the other horses following in somewhat of a straight line pretending to do the driving.

Driving cows using a "U" shape with the riders split into two teams with each team having their own cow.

We had to drive through each other's "U" shape.

We had to drive our cow around two barrels in a figure eight pattern while the other team had the same goal but went around the barrels in the opposite direction. We had to keep our cow in and their cow out.

The barrels were placed farther apart and we drove our cow until his nose touched our barrel.

The groups switched barrels. It was a race. We had to drive our cow through the other group and be the 1st to have the cow touch his nose to the barrel.

Riders formed into two touching circles and one rider had to pick a cow out of the herd and drive it into the other herd. Two horses acted as the "gate". The "gate" didn't open until only one cow was separated from the herd. The "gate" also had to watch to see that the 2nd circle of cows didn't manage to sneak back into the 1st circle.

We practiced cutting any cow out and then a specific cow.

Sage did well during the circle and herding exercises. Her cows didn't challenge her much, and we managed to get our turns completed in time to stop most of our cows from returning to the herd in the cutting game. The cows didn't run very far, so we didn't display our lack of impulsion. We did well in cutting out a cow. One secret is to sidepass into the herd, wait until the cows break apart and then go for the hole to keep them separated. This is repeated until you are left with one cow. Our sidepass is spectacular, so we did really well. We got several compliments from other people Saturday night. Also, several people commented on how interested Sage was in the cows. She always had her ears pricked forward and never took her eyes off the cows. I knew that there was a cow pony in there screaming to get out! *One extremely smart friend told me that Sage did the best of all the horses. (The man is now listed in my will)*

COW PONY - DAY THREE

Sunday morning was "COW EVENT" time. We formed into groups of three. There was a three-sided pen set up in the middle of the 30 acres. Our goal was to get our cow into the pen. My team was made up of a high level PNH certified instructor, who was experienced with cows, and a 13 year old girl. We managed to work together well. The teenager was too much in a hurry. I was too laid back, and the PNH instructor was perfect. We were able to talk together and resolve our differences during cow herding. Our first outing was relatively easy. Our second outing was "outrageously hard" and I started thinking about "hamburger". Our formation during this exercise was head to tail. There was one rider getting the cow into the pen. The remaining two riders "backed up" the first rider in a strung out nose to tail line. Where ever the 1st rider went.-right or wrong... the team had to follow. Our cow started out by making several sweeps trying to get back to the herd. We got to gallop right away. Sage cantered really fast...finally. We managed to get the cow away from the herd and took it right to the pen where it... squirted back to the herd! Part of the team thundered and Sage "pattered" after the cow and got it turned back. Sage and I were at the end and we got there just in time to stop the cow's 2nd attempt to get back into the herd. We were heroes!

Team members switched places, and I was in the middle slot. We got our cow to the pen again very carefully and... it squirted back. Two members of the team thundered after it and got it turned back. I arrived at the fast patter just in time to be switched to lead horse and rider.

The cow was successfully turned back from the herd. (Spotted Cow was smarter than our instructor had ever been during his faux cow impersonation.) This cow decided it was tired of that stupid herding game going to the pen. HA! It's little tail switched and immediately took off galloping down the fencerow. (We had learned that the rider has to gallop after the cow when it runs next to the fence line until the cow turns into the pasture.)

The cow was making tracks and I revved up Sage. She bucked. I used major force and away we went at a gallop. Suddenly, Sage woke up, discovered we were chasing Spotted Cow –her cow! We GALLOPED! (HARD GALLOP- Cowboy Movie Gallop!).

I was thinking about how fast Spotted Cow could run, the rough pasture ground and my impending death, but managed not to rein Sage back. I heard cheers from my team mates who were galloping far behind me, "GO SUSAN!"

I heard some raggedy cheers flying in the wind from the onlookers far behind us. Sage managed to almost catch up and we followed Spotted Cow thundering down the entire length of the huge pasture. I told Sage to slow down at the corner, expecting Spotted Cow to give up on this fence row madness and squirt away from the fence.

BUT NO! Spotted Cow turned at the corner and kept pelting down the new fence line. I gave Sage a slight body signal to run. This time she knew her responsibility and flew back into our death-defying gallop. Finally about half way down the fence line, the cow turned in and we all stopped to rest. I slowly pushed the cow to the pen. We were at the pen looking in. Spotted Cow had his head in the pen. I knew he was going in this time. Poor little Spotted Cow was tired! I pushed slightly by moving forward one step. SQUIRT! Away went Spotted Cow! Sage and I, just like all the movie cowboys, took off instantly in our now familiar death-defying gallop in a narrow outrun pattern. The cow ran for the herd. The riders were waiting excitedly in the line to keep Spotted Cow out. Spotted Cow ran straight at a horse and rider. Moments before, Sage and I, having completed our narrow outrun, was running full speed with the intention to place our body in front of the cow's nose and become the GATE. We galloped full speed two inches in front of the riders' line and oh so narrowly missed cutting off Spotted Cow. Spotted Cow almost ran smack into a rider in the quest to get into the circle, but the horse held.

Spotted Cow bounced back, not two feet from thundering Sage. The thought, "Death Comes Quickly" ran through my brain. I was certain Spotted Cow was going to bounce right in front of the thundering hooves of Sage, "The Impulsive Cow Pony". I expected to be astride both the Spotted Cow and Sage and be dead. Sage slid to a stop managing to avoid hitting Spotted Cow and the brave horse that turned the cow. Instead, Spotted Cow bounced sideways away from Sage, and cleverly slipped through a hole where its friends were waiting to celebrate Spotted Cow's endurance and cleverness. (Cow Hands- zero – Spotted Cow- three.

Everyone gave Sage and I a cheer as someone went in to get our cow. We were given one more chance. Only this time the team was allowed to form a "U". We herded "Spotted Hamburger" right to the pen again...but "Spotted Hamburger" squirted back to the herd and got to stay. "Spotted Hamburger" won by four points...but I ended up with a **RIP SNORTIN' COW PONY**!

The cow clinic ended. Asked what I learned, I yelled *"We learned to be a Cow Pony!"*

Sage and Parelli Level Two

All this time, I was taking about four hours a week lessons with Jenny Vaught. Gradually, I learned more and more horsemanship. Finally, we had passed all the Level two requirements except for the dreaded flying lead changes. Fox Trotters are not brilliant at flying lead changes. For one, fox trotters keep their feet close to the ground. Flying lead changes require suspension.

Do me a favor and start skipping. After a few moments, skip with the other foot leading. See where you need a moment of suspension to get the leading leg switched? That is exactly what a horse has to do except, they have two sets of legs on each end. Horses have the front leading foot and the back leading foot. The horse has to switch two sets of leading feet in midair. Really, try it. I've been in many a lesson with Jenny where the humans have to skip and do flying lead changes. On the ground torture is what the fat-self calls it. I don't have much suspension myself!

While I was practicing with Sage to get flying lead changes, I thought to myself… "Self, Would Velvet be able to flying lead changes easier than Sage?" During this long time with Sage trying to get all the tasks done and the flying changes, I have been silently bringing Velvet along too.

Why don't I concentrate on Velvet for a while and see what happens? Thus, I got two horses thru the original level two, except for flying lead changes. It turns out that Velvet was even more difficult than Sage at flying lead changes. I switched back to riding Sage and *whopaloosa*, she came through!

Sage the Brave became the first Missouri Fox Trotter to pass Level 1 and Level 2! This is an unofficial announcement because records are kept only of the people that pass the Level's test, not the horse nor the breed.

Let me shout it to the mountains! Sage is the first fox trotter in the world to pass the original Level 1 and Level 2 tests.

LEVEL TWO TASKS 1999

PNH Assessors:
Lee Smith 11/17/97 and Jennifer Vaught 10/18/1999

LIBERTY (Round Corral, Carrot Stick, Horseman's String):

- "Win" the Friendly Game with the Carrot Stick and String
- Drive the hindquarters 360 degrees, both ways
- Drive the front end 360 degrees both ways
- Get your horse to follow you for one circuit
- Play the Circling Game to the right & left, ask your horse to face you
- Finish with the Friendly Game
- Cause your horse to "smell his trail" for 10 seconds each side
- Hold your horse's tongue
- Simulate paste worming your horse

ONLINE (Halter & 22' Line, Carrot Stick & Savvy String)

- Play the Yo-Yo Game to back your horse over a pole and return
- Play the Circle Game both ways showing transitions of trot to walk and back up to trot
- Change directions at the trot, maintaining gait
- Go sideways without a fence for at least 20 feet, both ways
- Send your horse into a trailer while sitting on the fender. Count to ten and then bring him back to you without moving.
- With your hand on zone 1 (head), back your horse 20 feet
- "Push" your horse sideways for at least 20 feet

- Place rope around front leg; Play Yo-Yo Game and Lead your horse by the front leg (using 22' Line)

FREESTYLE RIDING

Bareback (PNH Bareback Pad allowed), Cherokee Bridle

- Mount your horse from a fence
- Trot a figure eight
- Canter for 60 seconds
- Bend your horse to a stop and make an emergency dismount

Saddle, Snaffle bridle, Carrot Stick

- Saddle your horse without touching the lead rope
- Bridle your horse from your knees
- Mount your horse unassisted

With Carrot Stick, leave reins on horse's neck or over saddle horn

- Trot a Figure 8
- Canter along arena fence, use Carrot Stick to make downward transitions: trot, walk, back-up

With Snaffle Bridle

- Back up in a straight line for at least 20 feet (nine step back-up)
- Trot a figure 8 showing two changes of diagonal
- Using a Casual Rein at the canter, show three simple (drop to a trot) lead changes
- Ease your horse into a gallop at least 30 seconds
- Come back to the canter to prove your horse is settled

- Still in canter, place your wrists under your reins and show four flying lead changes through a serious of "S" bends
- Slow down to a backup by lifting your wrists up into the air

FINESSE (Snaffle bridle, Saddle, Savvy String)

- While mounted, unbridle your horse (leaving bridle on fence)
- Place the Savvy String around your horse's neck and ride backwards, forwards to the right and left, return to your bridle and put it back on your horse.
- Go from Casual to Concentrated and obtain a soft feel
- Starting on the Casual Rein, show three Yo-Yo's from trot to backup using the 9 Step Backup Technique
- Back your horse through an L pattern (you can use logs or cones etc.)
- Show a full rotation on the hindquarters using the Direct Rein and Supporting Rein, one to the right and one to the left.

1999 World Celebration with Sage and Velvet

I dismantled my house and barn, packing for two horses. I arrived at the Ava, Missouri, Missouri World Celebration headquarters on Saturday afternoon. I had preregistered for two temporary stalls. I drove up to barn 2, stall 14 and 15 and tried to back my trailer perfectly aligned with my stalls. Then I tried to back my trailer raggedly to align with my stalls. Then I gave up and just parked alongside my stalls. I took Velvet and Sage out and tied them to the trailer. With pitchfork in hand, I went to look at their home away from home. Opened the door and, "EGAD! There was a horse napping in my rented stall!" There wasn't one human being around. The office was closed. Later, I learned that a mistake had been made when I was given the stall location. This was the year of temporary stalls and they were great. They were stall pens with canvas side, roof and back. They were back to back pens so the horses had a neighbor horse on all three sides that they couldn't see or touch.

Hoover and Me

I walked Sage and Velvet to the temporary stalls and we picked out two empty, unreserved stalls side by side. I drove the pickup over, parked, and we were home. Not long after that while I was making the stalls homey, a man drove up and stared at me. He seemed to want something, so I said, "YES?" He beckoned to me and tried to talk and just a whisper came out. I walked over to his car and found out this was Hoover Case, MFTHBA Manager, on the job. He was worried about parking and how the temporary stalls were going to work. I was put in charge of telling people where to park alongside the temporary stalls. Hoover and I managed the show grounds quite well, I thought.

All I Want for Christmas is a Generator

It was hot (90-100 degrees) and humid and I sweated a bundle. When I got the girls all settled in, I drove into Ava to eat lunch at the Sonic. I sat in the pickup air conditioning and rested. On the way back to the show grounds, I impulsively stopped at the True Value Hardware store with a rental business. Their sign said…"Just ask if we have it." I asked "Do you have generators?"

I drove away from the store with my shiny new rental generator perched in the truck bed. It was to go everywhere I went, from then on. I went back to my trailer, hooked it up, and turned my new horse trailer roof air conditioner. I'd never before used the air conditioner. Thankfully, it worked great. I settled down for a wonderful nap. Thank goodness for electricity and air conditioning made possible through generators (and thank GOD for porta potties. When I sit down to eat and bless my food, I always include porta potties).

The Week Starts

On Monday, I went into the office to sign up for my showing events. The line was minimal. I got up to the woman taking the information and sat down. She looked at my papers and then said, "excuse me for a minute" and left. I waited. I took a brief nap. I waited. I smelled under my arms thinking I had an odor problem. The other people made fun of me waiting for the 12th of Never. Finally, I shoved my way into the other line. I explained that I had been waiting a long time for my woman to get back. This woman said, "Oh, she's in the office counting money. You must have misunderstood her." Now we all preregister weeks before the show starts. No lines! Plus we get a $5 discount on every class. Every penny saved at Ava is money spent elsewhere at Ava!

My first classes, Amateur Ladies M and Western Pleasure, were on Tuesday afternoon. Tuesday came and I slept in late. I decided that there was no time for breakfast.

The Amateur Ladies (M) class is a performance class. Ribbons are needed for performance horses. Western Pleasure Classes are not performance. Ribbons are banned. Bridles for performance and Western Pleasure are also different.

There were about 3 classes in-between and I had to change bridles and get the ribbons out of Velvet's mane. I thought I could do that. Velvet had her bath and got jazzed up. Putting the ribbons in the mane drives me crazy, but I got them in. I got jazzed up. We rode triumphantly to the main arena.

There was not another woman in show clothes dressed up to ride. Instead there were a bunch of women leading mares. Hmmmmm. I looked at the show bill and thought, "I bet that (M) stands for Model, not Mare. Gosh Darn".

Fortunately, I have invested in a Model Halter and lead which are still waiting their first outing. Since Velvet is the most beautiful mare on the grounds, I'll just enter in Model. It's meant to be.

Velvet and I ran back to the trailer and I pulled off her saddle. Then I realized that I couldn't get to the model class in time. Being a mature woman, I gave up. I took the ribbons out. I put the saddle back on. I changed to Velvet's Western bridle and away we went just in time to go through the DQP station. Then I discovered that I had to get off. Since getting on isn't easy for me, I was upset. Someone said that there was a stool that I could use to mount in the warm up arena. Whew, more stress.

I was also about dead from no fuel for the engine (my poor foodless body). Nice and wonderful Ken Ragsdale carried a large paper cup of milk from the cook shack to near the DQP stand for me. Thank you Ken for saving my life! I think Ken intended on drinking the milk himself, but he selflessly gave it to me when I explained that I was dying.

We made it through the DQP. I used the metal fence to get back on. Soon our class was called and away we went into the show ring for the very first time at AVA. It wasn't very fun for us. We were lapped. We were dead slow.

What 360?

The announcer said "STOP". We did and I had Velvet back a step or two. I heard the announcer say "Turn Around". We turned and went the other way. After the class was over, a woman asked me excitedly why I didn't do the 360. "The 360?" I said. I didn't hear the announcer say that; nor did I see anyone else turn a 360. Aliens must have stolen my vision and my hearing or I was in a waking coma. I still don't believe it. I want to see a tape of that class!

Flashes of Brilliance

Wednesday afternoon was the Ladies Novice. Velvet and I loved that class. Somehow, in-between Tuesday and Wednesday, Velvet learned a faster fox trot. She got some "shake" in her get-a-long. During the class, we got in a multiple horse clump going down the straightaway. We were jammed between three other horses. It turned into a speed fox trotter race. We were all fox trotting as fast as we could, and Velvet was right in the middle of the pack. We all got spread out when going around the turn. I challenged them all to another straightaway race, but was ignored. We had flashes of brilliance during that class. Velvet couldn't maintain the smooth fox trot going around the corners so I finally figured out just let her do her "extended fox trot" (trot) around the corners. When we got to the straightaway, off we went in a speedy beautiful fox trot. I wanted to do that class again! We didn't place, but we had lots of fun!

Flawless and Fractured Trail Class

Thursday was the trail classes. At the last minute, I thought...Sage! Why don't I enter Sage in the 2nd trail class. There are two classes and I have two horses that are trail experts! I had entered Velvet in the amateur trail class. We were last and in we went for a flawless performance. We got a mighty ovation as we ended. There were three of us that gave flawless performances and I came in third.

Sage went into the more difficult Open Trail class. The back-through poles were set almost as wide as the horse. We had to be very careful not to knock over any poles. Instead of fox trotting between the obstacles, Sage hard trotted in the trotting parts. The sidepass through the poles was Sage's undoing. She was to keep either her front or back feet inside a 10" space bordered by poles. We did good going left and keeping her front feet between the two poles. When it was time go the other way, she was reluctant to sidepass. We were stuck there for a good hour and a half. That's what it feels like when your horse balks in the trail class at the World Celebration. I thought I would have to quit trying when finally she sidepassed back. I thought she did well, but my friends told me that she never put a foot inside the two poles. Hmmm, Ray Hunt, I'm going to have to "feel the feet" a lot better! There were just enough horses entered for Sage to place eighth.

The poles were in the practice arena all week. However they were set up in an "L-shape". I naturally thought the "L-shape" would be included in the trail class. Next year…get the pattern early in the week so there will be no surprises! (Years later, I learned to get the pattern months early.) This is what Pat Parelli calls "Prior and Proper Preparation instead of Piss Poor Performance".

There were more entries in the Amateur class than the Open and, therefore, more competition. It will be a good idea to think about entering the Open Trail class next year. (Years later, there are way more Open riders than Amateur.)

Versatility Events Entertainer

In the speed events, Sage elected to do "Half-Halt Gallops" as we went away from the crowd of horses at the head of the arena. It felt like riding a horse with three legs dipped in glue. However, when we turned around and headed "Home", we did run at a fast gallop! In the Stake and Pole Bending classes, we actually beat other horses' times. The Stake Race was unremarkable except the crowd was surprised to see that Sage could gallop fast after our "half-halt" gallop at the beginning. Sage felt no urge to leave the other horses at the head of the arena.

The poles were next. We sauntered down to the last pole and then, by heavens, we cantered back through the poles, doing flying lead changes! Sage has been in training with me and with Jennifer Vaught a total of 3 years to be able to do consistent flying lead changes. When I realized what Sage was doing, I screamed at every lead change, loud screams...piercing screams. We trotted back through the poles (away from the other horses), rounded the last pole and galloped home. I screamed all the way! It was exhilarating. It was the same scream that comes out of me on roller coasters. I became the crowd favorite.

When I appeared for the barrels, the crowd perked up. "What would she do this time?" When the Barrel Race started, one of my Internet friends found me and we were chatting excitedly. There was no competitive focus on my strategy for running the barrels. My number was called. I went deep into thought as to what lead we needed to start on...and away we went. We rounded the first barrel and headed for the next barrel at a gallop. Crowd Noise...lots of crowd noise. Finally, my deaf ears heard the words…WRONG BARREL! Whoops! I forgot the 2nd barrel! I yelled at the crowd, "I knew that!" and turned to swoop around the 2nd barrel. We then made up a lot of that lost time by going into our Half Halt gallop on the way to the third barrel. After about an hour, we rounded the third barrel and then galloped home. Really galloped! It was fast and I screamed again. Thank goodness there were only 10 horses, so I got 10th place!

During the rest of the Celebration, people told me that they didn't realize old people could ride fast and have that much fun. They were motivated to try the versatility events next year.

Costume Class
Hippy Chick on 60's Peace Fox Trotter

I got the idea to paint peace signs and flowers on Velvet using washable kids' paint. I partially burned a bra and mounted it to the top of my peace flag pole. I played Aquarius via my battery operated CD player and had loud speakers in a saddle horn bag. It was lovely music. Velvet had Salvation Army plastic flowers everywhere, but I lost a lot of them that were tied to her mane. She also wore the bib part of size 50 coveralls decorated with fabric paint with the words Peace and Love prominently displayed. Unfortunately, I put the speakers on the saddle face down and the on/off button kept hitting the saddle, turning the speakers off. But all in all, I made a complete circle (in parts) so everyone in the packed stands got to hear Aquarius (except for people sitting near the organ).My outfit was a tie-dyed shirt, sparkly bell-bottom pants, a pair of crazy salvation army shoes, a tie-dyed hat and a CHER wig. I looked like a creatively hideous flower-girl. Years later, I realized that the peace sign flag was upside down. Oh well, not too many people living in southern Missouri must have marched under the peace sign in the 60's.

The Costume Class was moved to Saturday night, and we rode in front of stands full of people. Wowee. Velvet and I placed 5th and the competition was rough. We had to ride against Elvis in his solid gold Cadillac,Tweety Bird and Sylvester, Knights in Shining Armor, Zorro, a Holstein Cow and some beautiful women…one on side saddle..another looking like a princess and a Hawaiian horse complete with grass skirts and leis. I heard a report that the Hawaiian rider tried to influence the judge. She had a lei for every judge. She was lucky not to be thrown out of the class for judge bribery. The crowd got their money's worth on Saturday!!!

PEACE!

GUNSEL

I had switched over to the thought of taking Velvet through Level 2 since I was having a most difficult time getting Sage to do lead changes. Pine Dell Farm sponsored Lee Smith, a certified Parelli instructor, to come and give a Level 2 clinic. The clinic was over and Lee had agreed to do some task assessments.

One of the million (original) Parelli Level Two tasks was to start from a halt to a walk, to a trot, to a canter. The canter is to be non-stop for 60 seconds and you are riding either with a bareback pad or bareback. After the 60 seconds, you are to come to a stop and make an emergency dismount. Well, poor sad Susan never got to the emergency dismount place as I couldn't get Velvet to maintain a canter for 60 seconds around the arena. You just have to love horses that go from fast to slow on their own accord. It's better than horses that go from slow to fast on their own initiative.

We "test takers" were a quiet, focused (some would say grim and scared) group. It was the Susan-and-Velvet partner turn to head for the rail and show our stuff for our assessment. We showed our stuff all right. We showed a three-legged trotting horse with a one-legged canter.

Velvet, The Princess of the Pasture, has figured out that it is a lot of work to canter in the arena and she would just as soon not do it. Velvet slid right down into a trot with a one-legged canter. This is where Velvet made her big mistake. The one-legged fake canter did not fool the assessor!

The first and second time we broke gait, I knew that my passing this task was remote, so I decided to get into it! I needed a spanker to get Velvet moving! However, all I had was my coat with the too-long sleeves. (I have short arms for my body.) I made one coat sleeve drop about 6 inches below my hand and I commenced swatting Velvet with the lightweight fabric coat sleeve.

How the Princess must have laughed, feeling that light nothing swack her on the behind. Then I started using my best cowgirl barrel racing noise; .shshshshshshshs!

Man o man. Oh little WOW…this made absolutely no difference to the Princess of the Pasture. We continued merrily along at our three-leg-trot/one-leg canter gait. Jenny was in the visitors stand and started to laugh as I went swishing by. But she looked over to see Lee Smith's mouth held in a tight grim line. Jenny just ducked her head and tried to disappear. I got to see all this happen because Velvet was not going at the speed of light at the time. I saw the grim face on Lee Smith, myself.

Then the rocket team zoomed by again…shshshshshshshs with that arm back beating the Princess to death…all .0000001 lbs. of pressure! This time Lee broke out in a hearty laugh and her booming voice called out to Velvet and Susan…"That's enough now, you can stop!" Ever the positive thinker, I yelled back, "Do you want me to do the emergency dismount now?"

Later we had to ride at a trot in two figure eight's with a Cherokee bridle… a rope with a loop through the horse's mouth. Miraculously, we kept up a trot without slowing down to a walk. As we came out of the last figure eight, we were to stop and back. We slid to a stop right in front of the assessor, and backed straight and true. Lee nodded, "Good Job" and was annotating my passing the task on the test sheet. I asked, "Can I do the emergency dismount now?"

Believe it or not, I never got to do the emergency dismount. But, I'd say it was that sparkling question that made me the hands-down favorite test taker of the day!

Greenhorn, tenderfoot, novice equal "gunsel" in the horse world.

VELVET DOES DRESSAGE

In June 2000, a staunch Western rider and Missouri Fox Trotter came to embrace the mystical world of Dressage! The words, "natural methods" in the description of a dressage clinic at The Natural Gait in NE Iowa excited me. The clinician was internationally regarded dressage instructor, judge and Olympic level performance competitor, Ellie Stine-Masek. Those "natural" words made Velvet and I feel that we might be able to fit into this ancient training system originated when men made war using horses. Yep, that's when dressage was invented-when men carrying swords went into battle. Men and horses had to communicate to get those battle maneuvers done. Dressage really means high-level training. That's it. We have taken the ancient training and made it high-level finesse communication. Pat Parelli explains that patterns were good to test military leaders. If they could remember a pattern for 20 minutes, they might be good candidates to command military maneuvers. Dressage started in war and continued until machines took over the war maneuvers.

Here's how Velvet and her rider's weekend went: We found ourselves in a clinic of traditional and non-traditional dressage riders. Velvet was on full alert watching for anyone who looked like they might sneer at the only rider that did not have to post! Ellie immediately found all the dressage "black holes" in all the participants. Funny, the holes in the Western riders were often the same as the holes in the traditional English dressage riders! Our group (made up of people from Mars and Venus) jelled under Ellie's constant sharp eye. Velvet was irritated when Ellie was watching someone else on the other end of the arena but repeatedly spotted us making various errors. Ellie would turn around and tell us what **I** was doing wrong, how to fix it, and then return her attention to the other side of the arena. The varied group found many similar problems and the exercises that benefited the fixing of all the riders.

We rode together in the mornings and in groups by ability in the afternoon. Here's what I learned: My horse appreciates "the soft feel" of true collection. (Of course, she also appreciates a loose rein.) I learned the awesome power of proper transition. Who would have guessed how much better the gaits are when the horse is prepared to transition from a walk to a trot; from a walk to a canter. Velvet's transitions have been based on speed without regard to preparation. Boy Howdy, did I have a different horse when the power of her hindquarters was harnessed in a frame of energy! Before this clinic, Velvet often had energy similar to a splatter painting!

During the last afternoon session, I (not Velvet) had expressed a desire to perform a leg yield canter, which is traveling diagonally across the arena. Ellie thought Velvet was capable of it, but we failed in several attempts. Then one of my biggest thrills occurred when Ellie rode Velvet. Ellie made it possible for Velvet to use yet more energy from her hindquarters. Ellie determined that Velvet was not ready for leg yield canters, but in the process, she made Velvet the most gorgeous performing horse that I had ever seen. If I could have died of sheer black horsepower beauty overload, I would have done it that afternoon, watching Ellie Stine-Masek riding Velvet.

When I got back on Velvet and cantered, I was shocked at the feel of the powerful canter and at the sight of Velvet's leading leg. I felt like I was floating atop of a graceful tank and her leading leg extended out farther than I had ever seen it before. I had **NO PROBLEM** deciding which lead Velvet was on as I saw almost her entire leading leg stretching out, gobbling up the ground! Ellie said this was because she had taught Velvet to better use her hindquarters.

All riders had similar powerful moments of improvements. It was the greatest of times! Velvet is now almost too good to speak to her former non-dressage friends. With a high head held nasal manner, she explains to them that she is now a *Drahsaaaahge horse*.

Velvet Passes All Level Two Tasks Except Flying Lead Changes

We concentrated on Velvet's Level 2 tasks. A year or so passed and we had passed all the Level 2 tasks except flying lead changes. I already had passed all of the Level 2 tasks on Sage except the flying lead changes. Velvet had caught up. Still, we were not successful in our quest for consistent lead changes. Neither Sage nor Velvet were successful at consistent flying lead changes. We were in Level 2 limbo.

Jenny had Velvet and me doing all sorts of things that make grown older women into strong resolute riders. Our favorite was jumping over a barrel as we tried to do flying lead changes. Oh the fun. The barrels were in the middle of the arena. Velvet and I would canter figure eight's. When we went thru the middle, we would jump over the barrel as we changed direction. Yes, most of the time Velvet changed her lead. We would fly over the barrel changing direction. Occasionally, Velvet didn't understand my wish to change directions. She would then get that understanding right before we crashed into the wall. How she always avoided crashing into the wall at the last moment is a mystery novel to me. Life went on, fun as always with group lessons. I love that life – group lessons with the same people.

You Can't Scream Outloud

It was group lesson time sometime during the horrid winter of 2000.

The "group" was standing in the middle of the arena with "instructor". Jenny was looking at each of us, telling us what we were going to be focusing on for this lesson.

"Patty, it will be jumping barrels for you". Patty shuddered. Jewell flips her rear end high in the air when she jumps…making Patty's body do a great impression of whiplash in action.

"Dale, we'll be working on getting the canter and the leads." Dale shuddered. Honey, Dale's new horse, is slow to move up to the canter and persists in using her right leading leg at all times. Dale is trying to love the canter. I could see that she had not yet attained that love.

"Debbie, we'll be trying to get Z to get into and stay in a canter." Debbie shuddered. The last time she tried to maintain the canter, Z showed the world that when it wasn't his decision to canter, he wasn't going to.

During this discussion, I was thinking, "Velvet and I like jumping the barrels, we always do great on our cantering or anything else for that matter!" I felt a certain prideful feeling of superiority. Without my brain functioning, I spoke up in a bragging whiny voice. It might have been a buzz saw irritating voice. "Velvet and I can do anything that you can think of. There's nothing that you could have us do that we can't do",

I had that superior feeling inside me and it would not be denied. I was feeling GOOD! Velvet is a perfect horse! I'm a great rider. Note to young riders: This is always when the horse makes you humble. If you stay humble, then the horse doesn't have to squish your pride in front of other humans.

Jenny's eyes narrowed. That's the only hint of temper that Jenny ever displays. Not many advanced students mouth off. Usually we learn at an early stage to keep quiet, have a can do attitude and try to be invisible when Jenny looks around to find a volunteer. Jenny loves us to learn and loves to give us challenges. Occasionally, we try to disappear in the arena so we can go along and do the things we are comfortable doing. Jenny insists on improving our horsemanship skills. She likes us learning to be better riders with more refinement.

Out on the wall she sent Velvet and I to join the group. She told me to get two carrot sticks (long fiberglass sticks that we use as extensions of our arms). She told me to put down my reins and use my body and leg aids to guide Velvet. I was to use the carrot sticks only if my body and leg aids did not work. We've done this before…many times. She told the group to stop and back. She seemed to be staring at Velvet and me during the stops. She had us canter, then stop and back. Velvet and I did fine with the help of the carrot sticks.

We were still stopped when Jenny came over to Velvet and me. She unfastened the bridle and took it off Velvet's head. I describe this as "ripping the bridle off". That's how I felt…like she was ripping the bridle off my horse. She was taking my lifeline away. Jenny "ripped" my lifeline away! Velvet had her rope halter on underneath the bridle. Jenny "ripped" that off too, saying, "I want you to look at that head and see NOTHING but her bare head!"

As Jenny walked back to the middle of the arena, she turned her head to me and said, "And you can't scream out loud!"

"Trot or optional gait," she directed. Velvet and I just stood there while I screamed silently inside. I always obey Jenny and I rarely talk back. Whoops. I just blew it big time.

Soon I got the courage up to tell Velvet to move. Move we did! We were able to stop and change directions. We were able to turn our hindquarters and forequarters. We were able to canter and go through the middle of the arena in a large figure eight pattern.

We also discovered errors that I had been making. One major error was to squeeze my leg against Velvet's side when I just wanted her to turn. I should have just been nudging her with my heel, because leg squeeze means "GO FAST"! Asking for a slow turn, I squeezed. Velvet suddenly careened at a high gallop speed through the middle of the arena almost running into a wall, before I could get my body and the carrot sticks to tell her to STOP! When you ride bridleless, the horse responds to your body and you cannot fix your communication error with reins! This might be called "the truth".

The final directive was to join Patty and Jewell in jumping the barrels in the middle of our arena figure eight pattern. I was not given any option. Velvet and I jumped the barrels bridleless! (Silent scream!!!)

What an exciting evening that was! I learned to nudge her side lightly when wanting her to turn. I squeeze when wanting her to go faster! Velvet and I both love to ride bridleless! We look Way, Way Cool!

Note: Both Patty and Dale were present in the arena the first time I rode Sage. Patty and Dale are members of the *"just like the old times"* club of life long happy customers of Jennifer Vaught.

SAGE OVER A BARREL

As her reward for being the first Missouri Fox Trotter to pass the (original) Parelli Level 2 test, I gave Sage almost a two-year break. She got to be the step mommy to JR and raise him. I rode Velvet in the meantime. Unfortunately, Sage chose to fill her stomach about three times as large as it should be. She got terribly fat on the lush Missouri grass. It is time for me to reclaim Sage back as a great pal and riding horse.

In the spring of 2001, Sage went to Pine Dell and became a pasture boarding horse. It's my goal to ride her almost daily for fun and to substitute her triple stomach with hard lean muscle. I rode her in a group lesson one night. One of our goals was to jump over two orange traffic barrels laid end to end. Sage has never really enjoyed jumping. Now that she is fat and out of shape, she doesn't want to jump anything. However, the goal during the lesson was to jump.

Sage and I ran over to the barrels to jump, but Sage chose instead to screech to a halt. She daintily tried to pick her way through the barrels. I sat and urged her on. I urged her on. Again, I urged her on. I looked down at the barrel...one of them had disappeared. I could see small orange patches sticking out from under her legs. I looked around at the rest of the group. They all were staring at me with expressions of great concern. It was then that I realized that I must have a problem. I did not know what it was. Jenny asked me how to get out of my predicament. I said, "Go forward! Jenny quickly said, "Don't ask her to go forward!" I took a quick look at the group's collective low-level alarmed expression. "Hmmm," I thought. "I wonder what the problem is?"

At the other end of the arena taking a lesson with Karen were green (beginning) riders. Before Jenny could say, "Don't touch the BARREL" three times, one of the helpful green riders RAN over to SAGE and PULLED the barrel out from underneath her! I frowned. My group's expression became one of horror. After the green rider got the barrel out from under Sage, she finally "heard" Jenny say, "Don't touch the barrel"! The green rider was alarmed and quickly PUSHED the BARREL back under SAGE! My group's, expression turned into major astonished horror.

However, Sage the Brave just stood there, not twitching a muscle. If this would have happened to most of the other horses in the group lesson, the horse and rider would have gone straight to the ceiling! Spook Up!

After this was all over, they explained to me that the barrel's open side was ready and waiting for Sage's back feet to walk into the barrel. Can you imagine what might have happened if Sage's legs got tangled up inside the barrel! Well, being Sage, probably nothing.

JOURNEY TO LEVEL 3 WITH VELVET

The task Velvet and I are focused is cantering around an arena bridleless and bareback. Velvet is to have nothing on her body except me!

Then (at a canter), we have to turn into the center and stop. The turn is the hard part. Last winter I fell off when she unexpectedly turned sharply at slow walk! If I fell off her at a slow walk, can you imagine how far my body would fling during a canter turn? The thought gives me nightmares.

Velvet and I have been riding full time in all group lessons, workshops and even on short trail rides with a bareback pad and nothing on her head. We look very cool. We try to pretend that we are not showing off, but we are.

A couple weeks ago at the end of the lesson, Jenny told me that I was not bouncing around on Velvet's back as much as I used to. You just can't hide stuff from an instructor, like off balanced riding! Month after month riding bareback, I got a lot better.

Heck yes, I've been doing better. I became able to ride more than a few steps without the death grip on the mane. I've been getting better balance at all gaits.
It's time to start riding without the aid of the bareback pad.

Tonight, Velvet was at the mounting block and I was ready to get on. Velvet has been moving a step or two during my leaping mounts with the bareback pad. I leaned on her tonight and she moved. We had words over that. Next time, she didn't move when I leaned on her.

I made my flying mount and she moved. I was able to hang on her side before I dropped off...on my feet. Velvet and I had words about this again.

We went back to the mounting block. I leaned on her, and she didn't move. I made my flying mount and was horrified to find myself VAULTING over her. Usually I have to make quite an effort to get all my upper body on the top of her back and the bareback pad makes me stick to her. NOT TONIGHT!

I vaulted over Velvet and landed on my feet!

Velvet and I were both a little upset over this, so I walked back to the mounting block on my rubber legs, sat down and rubbed her face and ears for a while.

Once again, I prepared to mount. All systems go. I threw myself up on her back and a muscle in my upper/inner thigh went SPANG! I cried out in pain and let myself land back on the mounting block.

I stretched out both legs for a while; went to the fence and mounted her from the fence...no leaping or vaulting involved!

After a while, I was able to ride her at a canter around the arena, turn into the middle and stop. My emotional fitness was just about peaked. My legs were illegally holding on so tight that my thigh muscle went into the spasm again. Thank goodness for her calm left brain introvert behavior and knowing to ignore the pressure of my legs squeezing her body in a death grip.

What a ride! Velvet did not break a sweat tonight. I am ready for the psych ward.

SAGE THE LESSON HORSE

After Sage and I passed Level 2, I took a long look at the Level 3 tasks. The one that stood out was "ride bareback at a canter. I thought about Sage's willful and strong left brain introvert personality. I thought about her past performance in bucking. I shuddered at riding Sage bridleless. I decided Velvet was a better candidate. Velvet is also a left brain introvert, but less willful than Sage. Her personality will make a better Level 3 horse.

What to do with one of the best trained Missouri Fox Trotters in the world? I certainly can't sell Sage. She got a year off for the foal when she became Nova's mommy. My energy is on finishing Parelli Level 3 with Velvet and bringing up JR thru Level 2 and Level 3.

At Pine Dell Farm, many people come to take lessons; People without horses, People who want horses; People with horses, but no trailer; Little girls with their mom and dad; People who want to ride a horse; Old people like me; Old heavy people like me who need a sturdy horse.

The need for reliable lesson horses is great. At the moment, the great need was to replace the first two horses that Jenny owned. These horses were the horses that every beginner rode when they first came to Pine Dell to take lessons. From four to seventy-four, students started out on these two great horses. Pine Dell has about 5 horses that intermediate to advanced beginners can ride. They had no Beginner-Beginning trusted horse.

I've been chatting with myself about Sage's life over the last several months. I decided to offer Sage to Pine Dell as a zero lease, lesson horse. I knew that a lesson horse was needed, but didn't realize that the beginner-beginning horse spot was missing! I was quaking in my boots about the responsibility that goes with such a horse. Sage is by no means a push button plow horse. She has very little opposition reflex left, but what would she do if someone got on her and started screaming? Oh wait, I've done that. I've screamed when riding her. She'll do OK!

We had our first tryout tonight. I rode a lesson horse and an advanced beginner rode Sage. Karen (Jenny's mother and the one who teaches most of the beginners) was very impressed with Sage. Everyone marveled over how smooth a "trot" she has. Karen said that some of her horses trot so big that she's afraid her beginners will bounce out of the saddle. Sage's trot will allow the riders to stay in the saddle! How pleasant.

Then we had the "Canter". By this time, Sage had figured out that the rider wasn't in charge. Sage was in charge. We had some nice laggard "'trotting" until the rider prevailed and Sage cantered. The rider exclaimed "How wonderful is this canter!" Sage eased into the canter instead of jumping into it as another lesson horse does...the one I was riding. The rider slowed to a walk and was told to turn and canter the other way. She slid into the canter nice and easy. We were all pleased.

The lesson was over and Sage is the #1 Candidate to take over the "Heart of the Riding Lessons" at Pine Dell Farm. Karen is going to start having Sage ridden by less and less experienced students until we get down to the real beginner--the 4 year old girl!

Sage will have a very important job. She will be very well taken care of. She'll get to come home on visits. She'll have a nice stall, great food and plenty of turn out, so she can live life as a real horse. I won't feel guilty because I don't have time to ride her. I am very happy.

Velvet and Susan at Equitana
Equitana in Louisville 2001

Jenny had found the love of her life and married Tony Vaught. Tony is a horseman and a farrier. He came to Pine Dell to shoe horses. Jenny talked him into changing his whole shoeing philosophy and start trimming horses' feet naturally. The feet are trimmed modeled after the wild mustangs' hooves that are trimmed naturally as they run across the great West. He also saw the great results Jenny was getting using Parelli Natural horsemanship methods. After he changed to her style of thinking, she married him. Using Sasha, Jenny's Level's horse, Tony went through the Parelli levels program became a Parelli professional.

The Parelli instructors were invited to accompany Pat Parelli and give demonstrations at Equitana in the first year. Tony's advanced horse was a stallion. They decided that Tony's stallion, Joker, might not get along with Pat Parelli's stallion, Casper. At the time, Jenny had her levels horse, Sasha, but they needed another advanced bridle horse.

A black velvety light came on in Jenny's active brain. She drew me aside soon after that to have a talk. "We would like to take Velvet to Equitana. Would that be OK with you? Velvet can be my horse and Sasha can be Tony's horse in the demonstrations. What do you think?"

Jenny had to look up to get my answer because I was hanging from the ceiling. My mouth was open trying to say yes, but my excitement innards had closed my voice box.

I posted this exciting news on the Missouri Fox Trotter Yahoo email list server and then was contacted by Missouri Fox Trotter people from Kentucky. They were giving a breed demonstration and wanted Velvet and I to do a solo act. Velvet and I were newly born as a horse performance act at that moment. Thank goodness the Parelli demonstrations and the Missouri Fox Trotter breed demonstrations were scheduled at different times during the four day event. Yee Haw!

I had to come up with a script and something to match the script. When doing a fox trotter demonstration, it's imperative to show the signature gaits of the Missouri Fox Trotter. I thought we could do that while our narrator told the crowd about the fox trotter's background, their great temperament and their smooth gaits. We decided that the two other people and I would go around the arena while the Missouri Fox Trotter horse was explained. Then the other people would either leave the arena or hide somewhere while Velvet and I did our show. I decided that Velvet and I would start with the flat foot walk, go to the fox trot and then canter around the arena. I designed my "specialty act" which continues much the same years later after many performances in many places.

Thank goodness Jenny was Velvet's main rider. She got her all nice and soft. The Parelli demonstration was in a huge stadium. My demonstration was in another building in a makeshift small arena in the middle of a million vendors and a million shoppers. That's what it seemed like to me. I did not get to practice in the little arena. I had absolute trust in Velvet. I knew nothing would bother her!

Our three-horse act went off really well. Velvet did not spook at the arena banners or anything. The other riders decided to get out of the arena, leaving Velvet and I on our show game! We did our three gaits. I drug a ball attached to a long piece of elastic. Next we did our fabulous leg yield fox trot and canter diagonally across the arena. Velvet has to travel both forwards and sideways. We did fantastic and the applause of the 300 or so people was loud! We had two barrels lying on their side in the arena. Velvet and I walked up to the barrels and sidepassed over them. It's something Velvet and I had been doing for years and seems like old hat. But the crowd was blown away. We had huge clapping. Then I poised Velvet about 20 feet from the barrel. I made the sign of the cross. The narrator asked me what I was going to do. I pointed to the barrels and made a gesture of jumping. The narrator told the crowd that I was planning on "JUMPING THE BARRELS" in an incredulous voice. I made the cross and prayed again. Everyone held their breath as Velvet and I trotted to the barrel. She leaped over the barrel! The narrator announced that she was "astounded that I stayed in the saddle!" I headed back on the rail and pantomimed that Velvet was upset to the announcer. I pointed to Velvet's bridle. The narrator translated. "Velvet wants her bridle off? What?" I took the bridle off Velvet and proceeded to do everything that we had just done, but without the bridle. I did not pray when I jumped over the barrel, but everything else was the same. We did all our signature gaits. We fox trotted and cantered diagonally across the arena. We sidepassed over the barrels, bridleless! Then we jumped the barrels! The crowd went wild! We were a huge hit!

Linda Parelli told me later that she was so sorry that she couldn't come and see our performance and thanked Velvet and I for being such a great representative of the Parelli methods.

We did our performance three more times-all with great success. I heard back much later from some fox trotter breeders that people came to their farm wanting to buy a Missouri Fox Trotter like the one at Equitana!

Velvet and Jenny at Equitana

Velvet had much bigger experience with Jenny and Pat Parelli at Equitana. The first Parelli demonstration was in the smaller 3000 seat stadium at Equitana. Every seat was taken, and people were standing. That was Velvet's first appearance in that kind of setting. The certified instructors and their horses first enter into the arena on the ground with their horses for the grand entrance. The music plays as loud as possible without blowing people's eardrums out. Their speaker system is high quality and built into the arena. The 3000 people in the crowd clap and scream when the horses enter the arena. The air is charged with high emotional electricity.

The music came up LOUD with a great beat and the instructors ran into the huge arena with their horses following. All the instructors did different amazing things with their horses. Three thousand people clapping and laughing charged the air even further. The energy level was on sky-high.

Velvet was jazzed up. Showing at Ava was not quite this big! Jenny asked Velvet to do circles which soon changed into reverses with flying lead changes. Velvet was leaping up, spinning the opposite direction and taking off in a canter. That was so cool. After a few minutes of doing on-line tasks, all the instructors took the halter and lead rope off their horses and kept doing amazing things, except their horses were loose. All eight or nine horses were focusing on what their human was asking them to do. Velvet was doing OK, although the big crowd, the rocking music, and the energy level, made her energy level come up to nine out of a possible ten.

Jenny ran over to the barrels. She positioned Velvet on one side and asked Velvet to jump the barrels and come to her.

Well, ha! Velvet was a little too charged up to be entirely hooked on Jenny. She decided jumping at liberty over the barrels was just too much and she took off! She went flying around that arena at a full gallop...tail up, mane streaming, head tossing, head high and ears up. For the spectators, this was a sight to die for!

All the other horses remained focused on their owner. Only Velvet was galloping around the arena. The crowd was enthralled. It's not every day that you get to watch a most beautiful spirited black horse gallop around, tossing her head...lookin' g o o d!

We have a game called the catch-me game. If your horse isn't looking at Mom or Dad and slowed down to a trot or walk, it's permissible for other people to run at the horse, chasing it away. The goal is to get the horse thinking that it's not safe out there alone with these other people and that safety lies with "MOM or DAD".

After a few more glorious moments of galloping around, Velvet started trotting around and the other instructors played the catch-me game with Velvet. When she zipped by, they ran at her, unless she was looking at Jenny. It was not but a few more seconds that Velvet looked intently for Jenny (and safety!) and then galloped to her. (Velvet knows the catch-me game rules!)

Jenny reached up to rub her head and the stands exploded with clapping. We had been treated to the sight of a beautiful horse galloping. We were treated to the sight of an invisible rope that bonded Velvet to Jenny in that arena.

Later Pat introduced all the instructors and this happened to occur when Jenny was riding Velvet around the arena bridleless. Pat commented on how people say that gaited horses cannot be in his program. He introduced Velvet to the crowd as a Missouri Fox Trotter showing that it's possible for a gaited horse to advance in the program. He told people that Velvet had been in the program for some time and was able to perform her gait bridleless.

Later in the program, Silke Valentine drove her scooter into the arena with her Friesian gelding running along with her. Remember I saw Silke's Level 1 tape submission when I was at Pagosa Springs. Silke is a paraplegic. Her horse was loose and followed her everywhere. Silke asked him to sidepass, backup, jump over barrels etc. He did it all and we could see the invisible rope that tied him to her. It was an amazing performance. Pat came out and talked about Silke's experience with horses. Helpers were putting a funny looking saddle on the horse. Pat told us that he had been training the horse. Pat said, "This is the first time for Silke to ride her horse." The crowd froze in their seats. Three thousand plus people in the stands knew a Kodak moment was coming. Silke told her horse to lie down. He did, right next to her scooter. Silke crawled out of her scooter and to her horse. No one in the crowd was able to breathe. We were holding our breath. Pat helped Silke get on her horse. He strapped her into the saddle. Pat and a helper hung on to Silke when she told the horse to get up. They strapped her legs into the specially made saddle. She was sitting on her horse for the first time in her life. The helpers stayed with her for a few steps and at Pat's signal, let her go on her own. She and the horse walked the length of the arena. Some people in the audience were sobbing out-loud. Three thousand people had tears streaming down our faces. Pat was crying. It took him a while to be able to talk. I don't remember seeing Silke dismount. I bet they led her horse from the arena while all of us were broke down in joyous tears. I'll never see anything to equal that.

When Parelli demonstration was over, Silke was sitting out in the lobby ready to talk to us. I walked up to her and started crying. I couldn't talk to her. She was puzzled by this strange reaction of her new life-long fans. I still cry when I remember this event and I cried when I was writing this story. Silke is a Parelli instructor in Germany to this day.

DAY 2

The 2nd Savvy Demonstration was held in Freedom Hall. That is the ultimate arena. This is the facility where the evening performance, the Mane Event, is held. You can be in the arena and look up at the seats that go to the sky.

The instructors came and wowed the crowd with the things that they can do with their horses. People were abuzz about this one and that one. Velvet seemed to be much more relaxed on this day. She stuck with Jenny until..well, that's the day two story.

Pat came in and explained some of the concepts. He introduced all the instructors and their horses. He did not elaborate this day about Fox Trotters. Upon introducing Jenny, he told the crowd that she was riding a Missouri Fox Trotter.

Pat told us that he was going to do something different each day. Today, he was going to demonstrate how these horses are horses...but also bonded with their humans. He is going to conduct an experiment. He proposed to turn all the horses loose and send them all out on the rail. We would see how long it would take before we could tell that each horse was seeking out its human.

One more thing...Pat's horse is a Stallion...a black stallion. Pat had Casper right with him when he proposed this game. I'm thinking...is Velvet in heat?

All at once, the instructors sent their horse out on a gallop on the rail. Eight horses went out at a canter or gallop. The game was to keep the horses going the same direction at the same gait. The instructors stood lined up in the middle to prevent the horses from cutting through any part of the middle. Eight horses went to the rail and started galloping.

The black mare was galloping easy...going a steady pace. All the other horses were going at a much faster pace. Velvet never tried to speed up and stay with the other horses. For five laps of this arena, we had the seven horses in a group and the black mare solo. It became apparent that the group of horses was catching up with the solo horse. On the seventh lap, the horses were all on the same side of the arena...with the large group in back steadily catching up with the one in front.

The slow, beautiful, black mare was about midway along the long end of the rail. The solo horse had started to become bothered that the other horses might have the nerve to pass her. Velvet is a dominant lead mare. She had started tossing her head and glared at the herd behind her. She was telling them "I am the lead mare and none of you better get too close to me!"

All at once, she whirled and galloped wildly toward the group. They were just coming around the corner. This was against the rules of going the same direction, but no human was fast enough to react and stop her. She ran pell-mell into the group of seven.

The group of seven became alarmed and slammed on their collective seven sets of brakes. It looked like the black mare "bowling ball" had made a strike. Horses went in all directions. Then, as if they had spoken to each other, all horses turned around and started running the opposite way, Velvet's way. This was Linda Parelli's end. She and a few other instructors ran down to the end of the arena to turn all the horses back the original direction and get them going into a canter again. This took several wild moments with horses going here and there. Bedlam might be too a description of this scene. In short order, all the horses had turned and were running the original direction. Jenny and Tony were relaxing on the other end of the arena...ready to fly into action if such an event occurred on their end. It did not!

Velvet was in the middle of the herd, but not for long. She dropped to the back and was left by the group again.

I was so thankful to have a horse that cruised instead of galloped. Velvet was so confident in herself that she didn't need to keep up with the herd. Pat Parelli looked at Velvet and you could hear him thinking, "slow horse!" I love slow cantering horses, especially when riding them.

Eventually the horses tired of running around and started looking for their humans to save them. Several horses came running into their owner. The gallop had slowed down to a canter and the group had lapped Velvet again. Velvet teamed up with Sasha. Velvet had ridden in the trailer from KC to Louisville with Sasha, so they had become good friends.

Velvet teamed up with Sasha and Pat started talking about them as the "married couple horses". Pat asked, "Are the married couple's horses ready to come in?" Jenny and Tony caught the eye of Velvet and Sasha and they came galloping in. Whoops, confusion occurred. Sasha wanted to come to Jenny. "Well," Velvet said. "the heck to this, I'll go to Tony!" Sasha went to Jenny and Velvet went to Tony! The crowd murmured, "They went to different people!" Jenny and Tony switched places after a few moments when none of the 5000 people were watching! The right horses were with the right people.

This is when it became clear to me that Velvet was going to do something every day to draw attention to herself. Velvet and my personality are more alike than I thought…drama queens! (By the way, the stallion did not cause one iota of trouble in the galloping herd.)

Pat talked for a while after that…and the horses rested. While Pat talked and the horses caught their breath, the instructors mounted the horses. Jenny asked Velvet to lower her head to the ground and mounted her by jumping on her neck, about the last

1/4 of the neck. Velvet raised her head and Jenny slid down to her withers and got her legs on both sides of her, mounting bareback...no halter, bridle... nothing but the small 6' rope around her neck. That is how she rode Velvet the remainder of the day two demonstration.

Day Three Velvet, The New TV Star!

This demonstration was held in an arena that was too small for the Savvy Team and there were not enough seats for the crowd. Many people had to stand and couldn't see very well.
Velvet was on DISH TV and Horse TV! Who knows how many people saw her at Equitana that year!

Even though the arena was too small to handle 9 horses doing their thing, they went in anyway. Since each horse is tightly focused on their owner, all the instructors managed to do the magic things that wowed the crowd.

Then Pat did some talking and demonstrations with his black stallion. After that, each instructor or instructor team went into the arena with an introduction.

Pat said that he asked the "married couple" to put together something nice. He introduced Jenny and Tony as they came into the arena and their horses...Missouri Fox Trotter and Quarter horse. Horse and Dish TV got to focus on two horses for the length of one song. Jenny was shocked when the song was over and told me that they had done only half the stuff they had planned...but oh well. A Missouri Fox Trotter became a TV Star!

Day 4
Pat's new resolve this year was to teach something useful during each Savvy Demonstration. He waited until the last performance

to teach flying lead changes. He and some of the students demonstrated the proper body position and drop to trot lead changes.

Jenny had improved my riding skills by giving me lead change lessons. Have I mentioned cantering as fast as the Princess of the Pasture could be motivated to go, cantering through the center of the arena, jumping over the barrel, changing direction shortly before hitting the wall and trying to get the lead changes. If you the reader would have been along for my journey with flying lead changes, you would pity me.

Let's go back to Equitana and Pat Parelli asking the instructors to demonstrate flying lead changes over two barrels. Luckily, Pat set this up to change leads from left to right. Jenny was relaxed as Velvet has been doing flying lead changes in this direction over barrels at home. Jenny was last in line to jump over, and failed to get the lead change!

Pat told her to do it again. Pat instructed Jenny to faster. Oh the million times Jenny had given me that same instruction! Velvet jumped and didn't get the lead change.

The crowd was straining for Velvet to get the lead change. Pat said, "We are going to get this Missouri Fox Trotter to do a flying lead change!" He instructed Jenny again as she galloped around. The third time she got it, to thunderous applause.

Three times Jenny got to ride Velvet jumping over a barrel. Jenny was so happy to soak in the attention of the entire crowd and Pat Parelli. NOT! I would have been thrilled, but the reader knows I possess the show-off horse gene.

I enjoyed this immensely. I took it as payback for all those times in the winter and summer that had Jenny letting me leap over those barrels searching for that lead change.

Before the flying leads episode, Pat had all the horses run around the arena again. This time Velvet stayed with the horse crowd. She never was separated from the group. She ran as fast as they did. When she wanted to come into the center, she came to Jenny and Sasha went to Tony. It was much smoother, but not as much fun!

Ah, sigh…life is good.

The Parelli team amazed the large crowds. Velvet and Jenny always looked fabulous. Occasionally, Jenny rode Velvet bridleless and saddleless in front of thousands of people. Pat Parelli always announced the instructor's name and the breed of horse they were riding. "Missouri Fox Trotter" was announced many times to about 18,000 people over the course of four days – two performances a day on some days.

MOHAIR CINCH HATRED

I love telling about the few times I fell off Velvet. The new Mohair cinch was one of those times. I fell for the great love that people express for Mohair cinches. I went to the trouble to find someone in America who hand makes mohair cinches. Nothing is too good for my Velvet.

I was riding in a lesson at Pine Dell in the indoor arena. The arena has corrugated metal walls. The tin wall has ripples in it.

I was zipping along at a canter and I felt a little looseness in my saddle. It seemed to be moving and not in the same up and down movement that I was doing. We kept going around a couple more corners and then the saddle felt loose, really loose.

I told Velvet to slow down to a walk as we went around an arena corner. Thankfully, the new mohair cinch waited until she really had slowed down to a walk. My momentum in going around the last corner resulted in the saddle slipping sideways. I could feel the saddle's desire to end up underneath Velvet. I guided Velvet close to the wall and tried to use the wall to keep me upright. My upper sideways body was leaning on the wall, making that huge corrugated tin wall racket that people from three farms away heard. Finally, the saddle decided that it did not really care about the wall propping my body upright. It fell off to the side. One of the facts of riding horse life is that where your saddle goes, you go. We had almost come to a stop at this moment. I fell right off into the thick wonderful dirt build-up next to the wall. Velvet stopped and the saddle slipped under her belly.

Pat Parelli says that prior and proper preparation prevents piss poor performance. The Parelli focus on safety for you and your horse meant Velvet was desensitized to nearly everything. This prepared her to ignore the screaming metal wall and the saddle going beneath her belly. I was not too far from being under her belly either. If she had taken off in fear, she could have easily broken several of my body parts. She just stopped and waited until I managed to crawl out of the dirt pile. I got the saddle off her, even though it was upside down.

Why do I hate Mohair Cinches? They stretch when they are new! That new cinch just stretched so much that there was no tension on it at all. I could have been riding in a cinchless saddle at that moment. Where in the new mohair cinch user guide did it describe this natural stretch of a soft Mohair cinch? Nowhere! I hope this prevents anyone who reads this who might be thinking about a Mohair Cinch. OK, Mohair cinches are great, after they have been broken in and stretched. I gave that Mohair Cinch away and have stayed with the same neoprene style cinch all the rest of my years.

BRIDLELESS RIDE AT MID-AMERICA SHOW

The Mid-America Missouri Fox Trotter show is a big deal. It is held every year in the same month at the arena in Springfield. In fact, the fox trotters have a Mid-America membership. You have to be a member of the club to get to compete in the show ring. All the best are there.

My friend Pat Harris had discovered me several years before. She is an excellent judge and volunteers at fox trotter events. This year, she was one of the center ring helpers. She told the Mid-America board about me. She told them how Velvet and I showed off at Equitana. She said that I had a half time act.

Indeed I did! I cannot remember the exact sequence of events. It's a two day event and my half time event was scheduled for the second day. The first day of the horse show was a class called Novice. Velvet was bored and needed something to do. We entered that class. The judge for that event was from our Kansas City club. Velvet tried to run over Dwight Hart, while he was judging the event. Velvet was smart enough to know that running around the inside of the arena is a lot less work that running on the rail. Poor Dwight, he was nearly toast. And you know what? He didn't place us either! The nerve!

I have developed a bigger act. Remember the movie, Men in Black? I've taken that concept and call it "Mare In Black". Velvet and I enter the arena, bridleless and I have sunglasses on. Hence, we are mares in black. We are totally sexy and cool.

I throw off the sunglasses and we do our three gaits around the arena. I call it, "Having a Ball with Velvet. We flat foot walk, fox trot and canter. We have the ball attached to a 22' piece of elastic. The ball bounces around and Velvet ignores it. Occasionally, it gets under her feet and she steps on it. Next is Velvet pushes the big exercise ball. She pushes it with her nose or hits it with her front leg. That is having a ball with Velvet!

The next part is Jumper Velvet. We notice the barrels in the middle. The announcer was reading the script when I was supposed to jump the barrels, but it worked out well because Velvet evaded the barrels. It is not like I have reins to force her body over the barrels. Velvet decided against the jumping effort. However, Velvet knew that she was destined to jump those barrels or never leave the arena. We turned around and jumped the barrels, and then turned around and jumped them again! Mostly everyone was amazed that I was still riding Velvet instead of eating arena dirt.

We managed to sidepass over the barrels without knocking them crooked. That's an art unto itself. It's difficult to sidepass a bridleless horse over two barrels and even more difficult to sidepass over barrels that are crooked or turned at a right angle! Whew…

Our next part of the act is American Reining. I have a flag and we do a reining pattern. I also put on a cowboy hat. I miscalculated on this ride. My reining circles turned into triangles, but nobody cared.

During one of my reining circles, I decided to switch the flag to the other hand during our canter. Unfortunately, I switched my hands right in front of my body, thus forcing the flag to be whipped right in my face! I was riding blind for a while. I tried to pretend that
this was part of the act, but the crowd knew better! We all chuckled.

Velvet did a reining horse sliding stop that made the crowd inhale and exhale a big ohhhhhhh scream with loud clapping.

Our last act is Dressage Velvet. I have a cardboard "dressage hat" that I found in a Dollar Store. I wear the dressage hat and Velvet and I travel at both a fox trot and then a canter diagonally across the arena. That is a very advanced maneuver called leg yielding. After the crowd claps and cheers, we do drop to a trot lead changes with 2-3 trot steps between the lead change canter. We are breathtaking!

I leaped off and the ring man helped take the saddle off. I asked Velvet to lie down, but she bowed. The crowd erupted into applause, thinking that was it. They quieted right down when I kept asking her to lie down. They erupted into applause when she did.

I petted her and moved to the other side. There was sort of an inhaled gasp noise from the crowd when I mounted on her. When she stood up, more intensive applause. This occasion was how I passed the Parelli bareback mounting Level 3 task. I sent the film of this demonstration to Dave Ellis and he passed the mounting bareback task. Yee Haw!

I rode around the arena bareback and bridleless to thunderous applause and it got louder as I was leaving the arena! I tried to turn and take "another bow", but Velvet really wanted to leave out the open gate. We did a departing reining spin!

After it was over, I was walking around the arena. I got many congrats and great riding exclamations from people. Many people chatted with me and exclaimed over the demo. I bask in glory!

ASSUME THE FALL-OFF POSITION

I've decided to save a lot of explanation and just have one chapter on the art of falling off. Firstly, there is no art or finesse for old overweight unfit people on the falling-off act.

The best thing you can do for yourself is to have played professional volleyball or basketball as a young person. Diving for the ball is a great skill for involuntary horseback dismounts. My body is trained to curl and fall on my side with my arm underneath, cushioning the landing. Do not try to reach your hand out and save yourself. Do not try to reach out both hands to save yourself. These actions leads to broken bones. If you are young and reading this book, go out for volleyball and/or basketball and dive for the ball. There is no greater skill that you could posses to prepare you for the older adult "splat". Oh well. I guess I just wanted to brag about playing Iowa Girls' Basketball in the glorious 60's two dribble, half court, six girl team. Sigh. Back to falling…

Occasionally, your horse decides to separate their body from your body at a great rate of speed and you end up falling on your back. It is helpful if you don't slam your tailbone on the ground first. Broken tailbones heal slowly. Keep that curl!

Physics explains that the rate the ground splats against your body determines the pain. There are occasions when you can nearly recite the Gettysburg address in the midst of your fall. Those falls are the "hang-high" Ker-splat. Other times you are in the middle of a sentence and then you are on the ground. That's a "no-blink" Ker-splat.

Here's how it feels. I've had a lot of time to develop a great explanation of "Ker-splat".

"Ker-Splat." Your body hits the ground. Incredibly, you feel nothing for a nanosecond. That's the splat part. Suddenly pain floods the section of the body part that hit the ground. There is no intense localized pain. Sometimes, the splat knocks your entire air supply right out of your lungs. No problem and no worry about breathing because the pain is uppermost important in your thoughts. In another millisecond, you feel the flood of pain radiating to your entire body.

You do not want to move at this point. You need to lie deathly still for a few moments, mentally checking to see if your body is going to stay alive. If someone is hovering over you, asking if you are broken, they might worry at the lack of sound coming from your vocal chords as well as the stillness of your splatted body. There is no air and it follows that there is not going to be any sound coming from your vocal chords. Air is needed to make sound and you do not have any air. After about a year, your body decides to breath. Automatically, you gasp and instantly utter, "I'm OK". You really don't know if you are OK or not, but at least you can assure those worried people hovering around you. They are relieved to know that you are alive.

Your brain takes a quick inventory of all the body parts. Body parts seem all to be equally painful. There is no overriding source of pain.

This is when you attempt movement. I generally roll over to and push myself up with arms and knees. If I can get to my arms and knees, I generally can stand up. Once when I tried to stand up, the pain from my shoulder was intense, stabbing intense. That's when you can diagnosis a broken collar bone. Morphine is needed at the hospital. I love morphine. Ribs often suffer in falls. However, no one at the hospital cares about broken ribs unless one of them slices a lung. Ribs have to heal on their own. You have to suffer broken or bruised ribs with stoicism. Even your good friends get tired of you whining about the rib pain.

I decided to try riding Velvet bareback one winter. I got on. Velvet took one sideways step and I fell off. I hung on to her neck as I was going down and ended standing up. That was my favorite fall-off.

When I was a young pre-age 50, I was introduced to jumping Velvet over barrels at a trot. What great fun that became. One summer day, Velvet and I were going for a ride with some horse friends out in the 40 acre pasture. I decided to show off to my friends how cool Velvet and I were. I had her canter up to two barrels and jumped over them. Her front legs took off in a high arc. Her rear end traveled straight to the moon. My rear end shot straight up into the air about 10 miles above earth. If I had stayed up there, I might have needed an oxygen mask. Velvet stopped and tried to get underneath me when I was floating on my 10 mile downward projection. She missed. I tried grabbing the saddle as I came down, but I could not manage to hang on. When I landed, I don't remember any pain. Maybe trying to hang on to the saddle stopped some of that "G force". I got back on and rode with my friends. Later Jenny explained the difference between trotting over a barrel and cantering over a barrel. "The faster one goes; the possibility exists that the horse will leap higher over the barrels," She stated. (Why was this not explained to me in the beginning?")

When Sage was a pacing horse, she often tripped and occasionally fell to her knees. While warming up for a horse show, Sage fell to her knees at a canter, My "seat" and balance had gotten a lot better over the years, proven by staying in the saddle instead of being "splatted" on the ground. It was then that I switched to having Tony be my farrier. He had taken up "Bergy Bergaleen's, The Hoofline Tells it All". Bergy introduced natural horse trimming to the world.

Another time Velvet and I were cantering along in the arena. Her body parts were way out of alignment, but I didn't understand that at the time. She tried to stop and failed. Instead she fell. I was riding an Australian saddle at the time with those polley things that stop a body from being flung forward. She fell and I fell right beside her. Inertia forced her to roll while my body was in splat mode. She rolled over my leg. It didn't hurt at all. The deep arena dirt absorbed her weight rolling over my leg. When I could stand up, Jenny asked me what day it was. For some reason, my brain had no idea what day it was. Secretly, Jenny called my husband. He appeared the next second, and I went to the emergency room. I had not fallen on my head. My head probably whiplashed and sloshed my brain around. The emergency room was full. I had to wait in the overflow room. Thank goodness, a horse friend nurse, Karen, found me and had me walk into my own emergency cubicle. It was painful to walk. We discovered there was nothing wrong with my head, but I suffered a broken tibia. I guess Velvet's 1000 lb. weight did cause damage to my leg. The tibia is the shorter bone from knee to ankle. Thankfully, it is the non-weight bearing leg bone. It does hurt when your tibia is broken when you walk. It hurt for about four cursed weeks.

I want to end up letting you know that you can't become a certified real rider until you have taken a Ker-splat. My first splat directed my horse journey to Jenny Vaught and the Parelli training. The rest of the Ker-splats were part of the journey to becoming a certified real rider. I highly recommend that you get further along on your journey before you take your first Ker-splat.

BOUNCING IN THE SADDLE MYSTERY

I do not remember how long I struggled around with the broken leg before I could ride again. I did not heal as fast as the doctor predicted which caused longer delay away from the saddle. You might not know this, but that adage about "get up and get back on the horse", has a purpose. A woman in her 50's or so falls off horse and breaks something is not a woman who heals and runs to the horse in a fit of hysteria happiness, mounts up and rides into the sunset. Those women are real cowgirls, probably 20 years old or so. I'm really an office worker. Aged office workers suffer from mounting fear the longer we don't ride our horse. This happens even when you do not have a broken bone. I was able to get back on Velvet and ride, because lesson times continued. Lessons force you to ride. I had a lesson in which to ride and then another and another. I was fine. I was the picture of confidence and balance. It was a "photo shopped" picture. I believed that I had confidence and balance when I started riding Velvet again.

My first lesson with Velvet had me suspect Jenny of trying to kill me. You see, she wanted me to canter around the arena and then canter through the center. I knew the centrifugal force of Velvet's hot blazing speed would throw me right on as soon as I turned into the center. Then I would be splat toast again.

I yelled something like, "Oh No, You're not going to get me to do that! " My tone was serious. I can still see Jenny's face – astonishment. Astonishment about this comment and be totally serious. I cantered around the arena and somehow the lesson ended. As time went on, I was finally able to canter through the center of the arena without fear of the "Ker-splat death".

I was riding Velvet and the young JR then. I would go up into the 40 acres and gently break into a lovely canter. Then my body would bounce in rhythm with the canter. My body wanted to bounce out of the saddle! WAZ UP, Body?

I asked my body what was wrong. My body explained that it just might be the saddle at fault. It was a recent addition to my collection. My brain pondered that for a few days and finally rejected that explanation. I had cantered in the same saddle in the past and never bounced.

Four months of bouncing in the saddle at the canter then passed. I thought maybe something inside me had changed and caused this bounce. I was clueless.

Velvet and I went to a clinic with Lee Smith. Lee loves to get riders to "feel" where and when each leg of the horse moves. She explained that she can feel either the back legs or the front legs, but never all four at once. She explained how the horse's barrel (the belly part) is like a bell when the horse walks. The back leg pushes the barrel to the side. The other back leg pushes the barrel to the other side. When your horse moves, the legs make the center of the horse's body perform like a church bell. Now, we are to walk along and try to feel each back leg move. Lee explains, "Feel the bell and you know which hind leg is pushing the horse's middle."

How cool is that? We walked along. I couldn't feel the bell action at all. I could not tell where each back leg was. Something caused me to relax and I felt Sage's bell "ring"!

I walked on. Turns out, I have to be relaxed to feel the bell "ring back and forth".

A big bell rang in my head. It was Big Ben. Big Ben said to me, "Self, you are bouncing out of the saddle when you canter because you are tense!" Self turned the Big Ben light bulb on and it rang loud and clear across the entire brainpan. "If you relax when you canter, you will not bounce!"

WOW! Four months of wonder resolved! Four Months it took to learn that my body was a stiff rigid object. There was still fear existing in my body and I didn't even know it. Since that Big Ben moment, I have to check out my body when cantering. I can canter for a while and then my knees try to straighten themselves. My knee muscles go rigid. My shoulders tense up. I start bouncing. If my horse speeds up at the canter without my permission, my knees and shoulders tense up.

Later I rode young JR in an all-day clinic inside the large arena. The next day was a lesson day. Every muscle in my back hurt. I'm used to lower back pain, not 100% muscle pain from the top of my shoulders down through my lower back. I commented to Jenny how sore my back was. She replied, "Sometimes my back gets sore too when I tense up." "Huh?" She must have noticed that I had been tensing my entire upper half during that clinic. We had lots of cantering in that clinic. How did she see that when I wasn't even aware of it! I thought I was totally relaxed on JR.

Thus, I learned to talk to my knees and relax them. I've learned to relax my shoulders and back. I have learned to sit back on my pockets and let my body find the natural balance point. However, if the horse speeds up without my permission, all those muscles are in danger of tightening up again. I don't think that I will ever be thoroughly cured from canter nerves!

Velvet Passed Level 2 Flying Lead Changes

It was a fine lesson day in the large outdoor arena at Pine Dell Farm with Jenny Vaught giving me a private lesson on Velvet. I had passed Level 2 Parelli test with Sage and was working on Level 3 tasks with Velvet. We do have lead change tasks in Level 3. The lead changes had to be done when changing directions after cantering diagonal across the arena. The canter is refined and collected.

Jenny asked Velvet and I to do some flying lead changes with loose reins using a large figure 8 pattern. By golly, we started doing flying changes. She did not have us stop until we got two flying lead changes in both directions. That was the lead change task in Level 2 that Velvet and I never accomplished. We did the task! I asked Jenny, the certified 3 star instructor, "Would that have passed Level 2?" Jenny affirmed that it would have. On the spot, I graduated Velvet from Level 2! Oh my!

It is not official. We did pass all the other tasks in Level 2 from a certified Parelli instructor. The horse is not registered as passing the levels in the Parelli system. It is the rider. However, we all talk about what "Level" our horse is. Velvet just became a Level 2 graduate, right along with Sage. I decreed it!

Velvet can wear all the graduate color strings with extreme pride. Those who know what the original Levels entail, treat Velvet with utmost respect and adoration. Velvet deserves all of it. Her journey was the longest.

VELVET AND SUSAN PASS LEVEL THREE

It had come down to the last tasks when Dave Ellis came to Pine Dell for a Level 3 clinic. By this time, I had probably ridden in eight Level 3 October clinics with Dave, all on Velvet.

My last tasks do not sound difficult, but they were difficult for a gaited horse with a lead-change problem. First task was to counter canter in collection around the arena. Counter-canter is cantering with the outside legs in the lead instead of the inside legs. When you are in a horse show and the canter is called for, your ride is ruined when your horse gets the counter canter or "wrong lead". Wrong lead is what it's called in the show arena for centuries. I did not realize the collected requirement until Dave explained. Velvet and I had progressed so she could dash around the arena with loose reins in a counter-canter. She zipped around the corners so fast that her outside legs could stay in the lead. It was difficult for her to manage the corners when she was collected up in a refined canter.

Dave coached us through and he passed Velvet and me on that task!

Next was the Four Barrel Run with lead changes at the barrels. We were out in the 40 acre field where Dave set up our four barrels. He told me the pattern and I blew it. I was too nervous to think it through. Thank goodness, Jenny was there to tell me the pattern and I was able to listen. We raced from barrel to barrel with lead changes at the barrels. I had the following attitude, "Level 3 or Die". It came in handy at the thought of galloping across a grassy pasture, slowing down, doing a lead change around the barrel and then launching out again to the next one. If I had not had the "Level 3 or Die" attitude, I could not have done it. I didn't even scream. We had several practice runs where Dave coached us through. Finally, we succeeded. My brain was numb and that was a good thing.

Our next task we are really good at and that is leg yielding at the canter. Again, Dave set us up in the field. We cantered from barrel to barrel, diagonally. Dave said it was the best cantering leg-yield that he had ever seen. Oh, wait! That was only in one direction. We have a tough time with leg yielding to the right. Again, with some coaching and practice, we got it. All the Level 3 tasks had been passed!

All the Level 3 tasks had been passed!

I gave Dave my task assessments list. Dave congratulated me on passing Level 3. How I kept from fainting, I'll never know. It took my brain about a week to realize the road to Level 3 was completed.

Velvet was done. She tried her heart out to finish this accomplishment. She got the rest of the year and winter off.

After completing the intense focus of my life for seven years, it was quite a letdown to get done. I felt rudderless! It was quite a while before I mentally adjusted and went on to other goals. A horse called JR was the new goal. That is another story a few miles down the natural road!

Pat Parelli and the tour came to Springfield, Missouri later in the year. He was told that he had a new Level 3 graduate at the tour event. Surprise! I was called out to the middle of the arena by Pat Parelli. Jenny, Caitlyn and Nichole were there too. Pat Parelli tied my new green string around my neck and congratulated me. The crowd gave me a standing ovation. My eyes were open, the sound was coming in and I was just stunned. IT WAS AWESOME!!!

Velvet was and still is the only Missouri Fox Trotter to pass the original Level 3 tasks! This is not official, as the Parelli organization does not track the horse breed that passes the task. But, I know it to be true. The Parelli world is a small world, even though it numbers around 200,000 followers. The Level 3 tasks have changed several times over the years. What Velvet and I did is a closed road on the journey of horse heaven.

LEVEL THREE TASKS

"Well Done" signed by Dave Ellis
Thank you Dave Ellis for the dedication, care and teaching skill that you put into my horsemanship journey.

LIBERTY – Round Corral, Carrot Stick, Horseman's String / Flag

Send horse around corral to the right at a trot	*Linda Parelli passed me on this task!*
Transition to canter. Show 4 laps	*Linda Parelli passed me on this task!*
Change of Direction to left with Flying Change	*"The first time I filmed this, I didn't realize you had to look at the back legs too! Velvet counter-cantered when we started doing this. Linda Parelli pointed out the part about the back legs needing to do a flying lead change too! Duh, who knew!*
Transitions to trot, walk, stop, back up	
Bring horse to you, Play friendly game with Carrot Stick	*You have to "own" your horse's hindquarters to get this done…to come into the center and be with you. (Linda Parelli passed me on this task!)*
Lead horse by the lip	*Linda Parelli passed me on this task*
Lead horse backwards by hocks. "22 ft line optional"	*Linda Parelli passed me on this task*
Lead horse backwards by the tail	*I used one strand of hair to show how light she was. That's "feel". Linda Parelli passed me on this task*

February 18, 2000- Here's the wonderful comments that Linda made on the video submission of these tasks: *"You're doing mostly the right things-just need more refinement. Stay inside your circle for downward transitions. Make sure you get her to value phase 1; that you fully execute phase 4- Step out into zone 1 and slap the fence. That door is closed! Don't be pushy through it. With the flying change, you just need to run back faster, push Zone 1 toward the fence (carrot stick and string rolled out*

> towards Zone 1) and then speed Zone 5 up. She gets lazy through the middle of the direction change and that's why she doesn't organize her feet for a clean flying change.
> Oh great and dedicated student, such wonders are you doing!
> This was really nice to see, you are making great progress. It just needs a little more refinement in the downward transitions and more "oomph" in the flying change.
> Look forward to seeing your next tape!"

I cherish these words!

ON LINE – halter, 12' line, 22' line, 45' line, 6" string, Carrot Stick, Flag or String

On Line was the most difficult for me. It took a long, long time to do some of these tasks. I didn't finish some of these online tasks until the very end of my level 3 journey.

With 45' Line	*The farther away your horse gets from you, the more ineffectual you become*
Show the Yo Yo Game-send your horse backwards and coming into you at a trot	*Dave wrote this comment on one of my failed submission: "Horse must continue backing. There's still too much opposition. Should go on out to end of rope." And another failed attempt: "This looks good-but let's see if we can get a snappier response so that all you need to do is toss the coils on the ground to back. For L3 you still are doing too much. Bring back was supremo!* My comment: I hate this task!
Send a horse cantering in circles over an obstacle course jumps, around trees, up and down hills.	*"Around trees? That means when the horse felt the pressure of the rope against the tree, the horse had to turn around and go the opposite direction. That takes a handy person to*

	manage that 45' of rope and a change of direction at the canter!"
Include a jump that is at least 3' high	
Back the horse up a hill	
Send horse sideways without a fence for at least 20'	*My comment: I hate this task. The sidepass had to be straight..no meandering forward or backwards. No rear end beating the front end. Straight down in a line with forequarters and hindquarters square. I hate this task.*
Send a horse into a horse trailer at the trot or canter and unload	*This means the horse has to enter the trailer at a canter or trot. They can't stop and walk into the trailer! Here's what Dave wrote on one of my failed video submittals: "Horse must continue gait into the trailer. Steady pressure to come out."*
With 12' Line and 22' Line	
Play the Circling Game with slack in the 12' line so you are circling the horse mainly by the flanks. Stop horse by pulling on the flank rope	*The 12' rope is attached to the halter. The 22' rope is around your horse's body.*
With Snaffle and long Rope Reins extended full length	
Drive your horse from Zone 5 forward in a straight line, then backwards at least 10 feet	*Zone 5 is behind the tail. I can't remember how I drove Velvet backwards from zone 5!*
Stand in Zone 3 or 4 and play the Circling Game, sending your horse around you to the right at a trot.	*Zone 3 is the mid section; Zone 4 are the haunches*

FREESTYLE –

BAREBACK AND BRIDLE-LESS (NOTHING ON THEIR BACK; NOTHING	

ON THE HEAD!)	
Mount your horse from both sides	*I can't even mount with a saddle by this time. How did I successfully mount my horse?**
Climb all over her, rub the rump with your legs and feet. ~~Stand on her back~~	*I laid down on top of Velvet and rubbed her rear end with my legs. We decided that I could be killed if I tried to stand on her back. Dave waived that requirement for me.*
Back her up 10'	
Walk forward, turn left, turn right, turn a full circle (pivot) and back up.	*The very first time I rode Velvet bareback, she moved one step to the side and I fell off! From then on, I practiced for a year with the Parelli bareback pad. Every lower level or foundation clinic Jenny gave and I rode in, Velvet and I were bareback and often bridle-less. Jenny decided when it was time to take the bareback pad off. I rode without it and was able to stay on! Velvet's hair became my bareback pad! That was amazing!*
Move up into a canter. Canter 3 circuits and top in the center	*Let me mention this again… bare bareback and **nothing** on her head. I worried about cantering and turning into the middle. There is such a thing as centrifugal force. But, after a while, I could stay on, even when she turned at a canter. Yes, I was amazed!*
Snaffle Bridle, Saddle, Two Carrot Sticks	
Back your horse up in a straight line for at least 10 feet	
Transition from halt to canter	*To say this another way: From a halt start cantering! There is no walking or trotting in-between!*
Show three simple (drop to a trot) lead changes	*Here's what Dave Lichman wrote in a failed video submittal: These are still simple changes..one or two*

	steps of gait in-between. Continue this process — slower (here's where three speeds at the canter come in) and more elevated until the change happens directly
Ride over two jumps that are at least 2 ft high	Let me mention again that I was holding two carrot sticks. That means you are not holding on to your reins. You have a bridle on your horse, but you can't use it! It's difficult to hold on to the western saddle horn too when you are holding a carrot stick in each hand while sailing over those jumps! In a level 3 clinic that I audited a long time before I was ready for this, I watched a guy holding two carrot stick jump over a barrel and he ended up sitting in front of his western saddle — without injury. Think of what his body had to do to end up there! That was pure entertainment for the lucky auditors!
Canter to the assessor in a straight line and come down to a back up.	
ON A CASUAL REIN	At least I could hang onto my reins for this one!
GALLOP a Barrel Pattern with four barrels. Show two turns to the right and two to the left. Stop your horse in the middle of the barrels and come down to a 9 step back up	This was one of the last three tasks that I passed where I had the attitude of "Level 3 or Die. Dave had me do this out in a big grassy field. GALLOP! SCREAM! Dave expected flying lead changes around the barrel. We were to slow down to a CANTER for the turns around the barrel and accelerate back up to a gallop. See what I mean about Level 3 or DIE!

	Dave's Comments on this: Good balance and harmony with your horse. You recognized your horse's space and capability nicely, Dave Ellis

FINESSE – Snaffle Bridle, Saddle, 45' line, Kite String

With Contact and a Soft Feel	
Show a slow, medium and fast walk	
Show a slow, medium and fast trot	*The assessor was someone other than Dave Ellis. He told me that this was the best that he had ever seen this task performed. The Missouri Fox Trotter has the flat foot walk, the fox trot and the real trot. That's what I used for this task!*
Show a slow, medium and fast canter	
Come down to a graceful halt and back up	*I had contact with my horse's mouth. All I did was change my body position to "back". Velvet stopped and backed with little hesitation between the halt and back up.*
Drop Reins and Stand Still	*Velvet loved this task. There's no fancy moving jig steps at this stage of the game!*
Obtain a soft feel	*Pick up the reins and the Velvet "gives to" the light pressure.*
Move your horse's right front leg and then left hind leg	*No other leg gets to move. This is a literal translation. It takes a mirror to figure this out until you can feel every step that your horse takes! I didn't have a mirror.*
Rock her backwards and forwards and side to side	*This is called Dancing with your horse! It means shifting her weight, not taking a step!*

Ride from a backup into a canter and back down to a backup three times. Canter Yo Yo	*Oh this is difficult*
Ride a serpentine at the canter showing three simple changes thru the walk	*Canter and drop to walk and then pick up the other lead.*
At the canter, cause your horse's hindquarters to come in off the track while the forehand travels straight.	*During a live assessment with Dave he said, "Susan, I don't see Velvet move her hindquarters off the track at all!" We failed that round.*
Pick up a right lead. Demonstrate a counter canter to the left (maintain right lead) on a full circle	*Velvet could only do this at a fast canter with loose reins. We couldn't hold the counter canter in a circle. This was one of the last tasks that we passed with Dave's help and coaching.*
Trot your horse in a figure eight showing two changes of diagonals.	*This means I had to post. Posting on a smooth gaited horse is more difficult as there is no suspension to lift you up.*
Trot your horse diagonally sideways across a space of at least 25'	*We had to do this at a flat foot walk. Doing this while fox trotting made Velvet pace. Yeccha! Velvet would much rather canter diagonally than anything else!*
Canter your horse diagonally sideways, on the left lead, across a distance of at least 25 feet	*We got really, really good at this. We are breathtaking at this*
Show a flying change from left to right, cantering diagonally sideways to the right then show another flying change from right to left.	*The flying change was very difficult for Velvet with a concentrated rein. This was one of the three last tasks.*
Bring your horse gracefully down to a backup	*Piece of cake!*
Using the 45' line	
Drag a log or tire, etc, while riding your horse. Drag it forwards for 30 feet then turn and face it.	

Drag it while backing your horse for another 15 feet	
Dismount your horse and ask her to back up with your reins, causing her to drag the obstacle a little backwards and hold it while you go and pet the object	*We drug a barrel. Yes, I had to go and pet the barrel while Velvet held the barrel still.*
Bring her forward while you are at the object and untie the 45' line	
Mount your horse and gather up your rope	*I had to do this so Velvet ended up at the mounting block so I could get on. I failed it the first time because I didn't gather up my rope in a loop. It was a mess. Level 3 people learned to love their rope or fail. I failed this twice! The third submission is when I finally passed this task!*
Using a 9' length of Kite String	
Take your bridle off while mounted and place the kite string in your horse's mouth. Walk, trot and canter a circle and then come down to a backup.	*There had to be light contact with your horse's mouth. This was to show that your horse's head set was light enough to be refined, even with a kite string. I found a heavy duty kite string that helped.*
Dismount, rub your horse on the head, then turn and leave with your horse following you freely.	
Overall picture of rider's refinement (includes subtlety of communication, independent seat, gracefulness	

My Dream Come True

In October, 2008, I rode Velvet with our demonstration skit in the Missouri Women and Horses Expo Versatility three day completion. The third day was freestyle and I was awarded nearly all possible points for that day. I thought that was a dream for Velvet and I, but read on to learn about the next year!

July 2009 was my bucket list fulfilled. July 2009, I got the one thing that I wanted to put my grand wish to bed and the forever-be-happy dream made into reality!

Velvet and I got to do our routine in front of Pat Parelli, Walter Zetl, Pat Parelli master students, Jenny Vaught and the Vaught extended family and a crowd of nearly a thousand people. In my world, this is when you climb Mount Everest and the angels sing HALLELULA!

In 2009, Pat Parelli decided his tour would be part teaching and part watching what his loyal Parelli students can do. It's the Parelli Games judged. Guess who was the judge? Mr. Pat Parelli himself!

There were different categories of student participation. Velvet and I chose freestyle. We embody Freestyle. We are Freestyle. We can do just a little bit of everything and we can do it with perfect communication. Velvet understands perfectly what I want and thankfully, she did it for me on my dream-come-true day.

Having a Ball with Pat Parelli: (no hat)
I had rigged up the ball attached to the 20' elastic ¾ thread. We pull the ball and it bounces all over the place. I set up my helpers on the outside of the arena. They each have a medium size play ball. Velvet and I make our grand entry into the arena, pulling our bouncing ball. Each helper tosses us a ball as we zip by and I bat it back to the helper. At the end of our second round, our attached ball was stepped on a few times and deflated. We threw the empty elastic string to a helper. When the 2nd round was done with the batting of the balls, we go into our "Having Barrels of Fun with Pat Parelli" phase.

Velvet and I lined up in front of barrels lying side by side. I lifted my legs out of the saddle and leaned back until my hand touched Velvet's rear, right where the tail starts. This is the Linda Parelli certified "find your balance point" maneuver. With my pockets deep in my saddle and my balance point procured, I offered a prayer and sign of the cross. We then, yes! We jumped the barrels and then we turned around and jumped them again! The crowd roared, clapped and laughed! Oh the crowd was having a good time!

Velvet and I started to phase into the next act. We ran over to Jenny and I got my find cowgirl hat on and got my red retracted umbrella.

"Raining" Pattern– Get Your Cowgirl Hat On!
Velvet and I love the Reining / Raining Pattern. Our red little umbrella makes reining into raining!. We cantered in our reining horse circles and then went around the corner of the arena. As we were cantering along, I extend the umbrella. Click, click it goes until it's fully extended. As we were running down the long side of the arena, I press the umbrella button! The umbrella whooshes open. I held it up while still in our run and it turned inside out. We slid to a stop with the red umbrella inside out! Oh so cool. The crowd was on their feet, screaming, clapping and laughing. Guess they had never seen a reining / raining pattern

quite like ours! We rode once around the arena with the umbrella for a while getting it turned inside and right side out, depending on which way I pointed the umbrella! That was fun. Reining, Raining pattern! The crowd was hysterical and was time to go to our third phase. We ran over to Jenny again and traded the cowgirl hat for the cardboard dressage derby.

Dressage – Get your Dressage Derby ON!

It's the same cardboard dressage hat that I found in a convenience store long ago. It fits perfectly. It's stapled together. I'm going to be devastated when time makes it into mush. I really need a real dressage hat before my beloved cardboard hat disintegrates.

I put on my dressage hat and get the Parelli carrot stick, AKA, orange dressage whip. We become Dressage Queens! My nose automatically raises and we look down upon the "commoners" in the crowd. I did the dressage queen snort several times just to let people know how important we have become. Walter Zetl laughs! I was hoping the "dressage god of the Western world" would find humor in my parody of a dressage queen! Whew!

First we leg yield trot and then we leg yield canter diagonally down the long end of the arena. Wowsa Dowsa! The crowd stands, cheers and claps again.

My music ends and Velvet and I stand there, getting our breath! Pat Parelli speaks into his microphone: *"Susan Engle, If I didn't have boots on, you would have blown my socks off! You got 10 in all four categories. Your ribbon is the top ribbon - Level 5 in performance!"*

Velvet and I got more standing ovations from the crowd as Pat hands me our blue ribbon! He said some more nice things to me.

My former horse, JR, had been in a spotlight the day before with Chris Wolters. Chris is a Downs Syndrome young man. He and JR have an incredible bond. JR did so wonderful for Chris that it brought everyone to tears in that auditorium. Pat awarded Chris a Level 1 Ribbon on the spot and pronounced him to have passed Level 1. Pat had learned that JR used to be my horse for a number of years and complimented me on JR being a wonderful example of what Love, Language and Leadership will make happen.

Pat told me to go show off to the crowd! Velvet and I floated out of the arena to more standing ovations and cheers. We didn't hurry out of the arena either! WE SOAKED IT UP!

Now that's the way a dream should end! Oh, I forgot to mention: Velvet was bridleless during this entire demonstration! BRIDLELESS in The American Royal Hale Arena! I rode for Pat Parelli, his instructors, his master class students and a crowd of nearly 1000 people. That's the way to end the first story of my dream with horses journey!

The next day, Nichole Copple rode Velvet in a routine along with her sister on Sasha for Pat Parelli. Again, Velvet was awarded a Level 5 ribbon along with Nichole. Velvet was a rock star that weekend. I was too. I gave hope to a lot of women who look like me. You can do it. You can have your dream of riding your horse like your horse genes want. Horse genes can win through!

Later in the year 2009, Nichole Copple rode Velvet to multiple World Grand Championships at the Missouri Fox Trotter World Celebration. Nichole and Velvet are World Grand Champion Youth Ranch Horse and Versatility Horse. 2009 was a fabulous year.

Horse Genes said, "Susan, we knew you could do it! Thanks for the taking the journey."

Jenny's Chapter and then Tony too!

Jennifer Vaught deserves her own chapter. Jenny has become my best friend forever. She has always been kind and understanding. She always listens and sees things from your point a view. She takes the time it takes to develop the dream you have with horses. She has taken a lot of time to develop my dream. I have traveled with her. I have hosted her clinics. I have seen more beginning clinics than anyone except instructors. During her Parelli years, I missed only a few clinics. I've participated in most of her clinics and watched the ones where I didn't participate. She is a most wonderful person.

I have watched her raise her family. She uses natural horsemanship to raise her family. Her children are wonderful, obedient, hardworking and hard playing. They know how to fill their outdoor time with games and make believe. Nichole and Caitlyn are following Jenny and Tony in the love and training of horses. Justin is going to be our mechanic to fix everything. Baby Aaron, we don't know what he's going to be yet, but he will be entertaining! He loves to ride in the saddle with either his mother or father and that's where he takes his naps. We are hoping for an Aaron cowboy.

Jenny married Tony during this book. Natural horsemanship is at the core of their existence along with their deep Christian faith. My horsemanship and my human-ness has blossomed under their leadership, skill with horses and their example of how they lead their lives.

All my horses have been started or trained by Tony and Jenny Vaught. I cannot imagine riding a horse that hasn't been trained by them. My life flashes in front of my eyes at the thought. They have kept me safe since 1994 and that is quite a record in the horse world!

As of this writing, Tony and Jenny are training horses and people at For the Horse Ranch located 30 miles north of Springfield. The website is http://www.forthehorse.org. Please contact them to start training you and your horse. I always say that giving your horse the start with Tony and Jenny is the best gift that you can give to yourself and your horse. Please join me in clinics and lessons with Tony and Jenny. Sometimes I get to tell my stories in real life. Sometimes you get to see my newest story developing in real life. As of this writing, I'm starting to develop my sixth horse in another journey from young horse to finished horse.

Personality and Horse Breed For Beginning Older Adult Rider

I got lucky with my horse choices, both with their personality and their breed. I asked all my Missouri Fox Trotter friends for reasons to own a fox trotter. Rick Watson gave me a great list of reasons:

Of all the possible horses to claim as the best, it's the Missouri Fox Trotter;

- which have the ability to compete with quarter horses in reining, cutting, and yet compete with a Walking horse for a pleasure ride on the trails;
- which are sure footed by the nature of the diagonal gaits but still have the naturally smooth ride of a gaited horse;
- which are able to compete with the Arabian on an endurance competition but provide a novice the ability to ride for miles without saddle sores because of the natural ride;
- which provide those suffering with back pain an option to ride and also provide retraining for the minds of developmentally delayed children because the foxtrot has the same natural rhythms as the crawl of a baby who is learning muscle coordination and cross brain communication;
- which provide any one regardless of financial ability the ability to own and personally train a show horse that will be able to show on a world stage and possibly win ribbons at the world class show without spending more on the horse than on the pick-up that pulled the horse to the show.

All breeds have beautiful animals and some individuals that can warm the darkest day with the understanding that "what is good for the outside of a horse is great for the inside of a man".

If you are honest and evaluate the above criteria you are left with the narrow field of one --the FOX TROTTER

This was true for me at the age of 24 when I made this decision and is true today at more than twice that age

"Why, because by 40 we have the wisdom to."

Rick Watson
formally known as "Uncle Albert"

MISSOURI FOX TROTTER

We talk about horse's spirit. We talk about hot and cold breeds. Let's use a scale from 1 to 10 and cold to hot. One would be a draft horse and ten would be an Arabian or a Saddlebred. Draft horses were not bred to race across the dessert. A draft horse is bred to pull plow and wagons. The spirit is there, but it's not a "race the wind" kind of spirit like the Arab. The Arabian horse has a high spirit. Arabians are on the eight to ten category.

The older beginning adult rider needs to get a horse that doesn't think about "racing with the wind". Horse breeds can be grouped according to generalities. Not all of them fit into the bell curve, but generally the Missouri Fox Trotter is about a three to four in spirit. I like that a lot. I call that "safe".

Let's talk about the physical impact of a horse on the older adult's body, especially us partially fit bodies. A Missouri Fox Trotter who does the signature gait has no suspension. Your body is not jolted up and down.

People with back problems really enjoy the gaits. Your lower back is stretched. It gets moved back and forth instead of bang-up-and-down. Suspension gaits like the trot, causes bounce which can greatly irritate the lower back. Many baby boom riders switch to a gaited horse because of back problems. Fox Trotters are pain pills on four legs. They are just a little more expensive that Aleve! You don't have to ruin your liver with pain pills if you would just ride a fox trotter with the signature gaits.

Let's talk about bounce. When you first get a horse, your balance is not the best. When you bounce up and down, it is easy to get off-center and feel like you are going to bounce off. This is not a good feeling. Missouri Fox Trotters enable you to feel comfortable in the saddle while your "seat" is learning how to balance and be with the horse. I've had skinny little 20 year old girls tell me they wish they could ride as well as I can. I am always speechless when that happens. I figure skinny girls have perfect balance because they are thin. I guess that is not the case. I'm still amazed. I wish I could ride at this age and be skinny. I'm still trying the "D"iet word.

Let's talk about curvy cowgirl adult women riders. We have masses of body parts, particularly above the waist. These things bounce when riding a trotting horse. It's pretty awesome to watch the front of curvy women when riding high stepping horses.

There are ways we women try to avoid this spectacle. Some of us wear double or triple "garments" to stop the humiliating bounce. Others try to keep the parts in place with elastic wrap bandages. We try to bind the bouncing body parts, We can buy really expensive undergarments that cut into your rib and backbone to keep our parts from bouncing. I have one of these undergarments with front hooks and it takes two helpers to get the hooks fastened. I was at a horse show once and just had bought this garment. It was too uncomfortable to wear all day, so I decided to put it on at the horse show. I got it on over my head at home, with the hooks already fastened. At the August horse show in my hot trailer, my skin was too moist for the garment to slide down from my shoulders. I unfastened some of the hooks and got it partially where it should be. But I had to call for help and that was one of the most embarrassing situations of my life. One of my friends had to see me, exposed, and struggling to get the undergarment pulled down and hooked. That person had to fasten some hooks on my front! That memory causes me to shudder in agony to this day.

With my Missouri Fox Trotter, I can wear ordinary undergarments and not make a spectacle of myself. I would tell you a secret about not wearing any undergarment in the cold winter days when I have on at least two layers of sweaters and coats, but that would be embarrassing.

After you have your hysterectomy or vasectomy, you can ride a lot sooner if you have a smooth gaited Missouri Fox Trotter.

I asked my men friends over forty why they ride a Missouri Fox Trotter.

Paul said he rides a fox trotter because he looks and feels sexy. Now that I think about it, he's right.

Keith said, "Because:
1. I like finishing well in endurance.
2. Because my Pooles Blue Boy horse, Blues Golden Lad, ALWAYS leave me with a smile when I ride him.
3. Because pretty women ride Mfts.
just saying …

I like Keith a lot. I think what he says about pretty women riding Missouri Fox Trotters is absolutely true, just thinking about me for example!

Get a Missouri Fox Trotter with the signature gaits and be comfortable!

Jeannie pointed out that gaited horses were in those old time cowboy movies. Movie producers knew back then that their cowboys should not bounce into the sunset. Watch those horses in the black and white old movies. You likely will see a fox trot, running walk or flat foot walk. Cowboys didn't post and they didn't bounce. Thank your gaited horse for that!

Another piece of luck for me is that I picked two left-brain introverts to start my riding career. Introverts don't like to move their feet. Left-brain introverts are my favorite personality. I like to convince horses to move their feet rather than to have their feet take me at speeds and places I don't want to experience. Shudder.

Follow the Parelli program. The program gives you attainable goals, confidence and keeps you safe. The levels tests in this book are no longer being used. It's much easier to advance through the program now. The tasks are more suitable to how people progress, particularly the beginning unfit adult rider! You will still get to the tasks outlined in Level 3, but you have smaller steps to take to get there. Many of the tasks listed in this book have been raised to higher levels.

Get Jenny and Tony Vaught to train your horse! Join me in the group lessons as I start another journey with another horse. After all, I need more stories to keep writing more books!

Susanality aka Humanality

How do you communicate with another species? How do you communicate with a non-verbal species that instinctively remembers long ago forefathers being chased and eaten by lions? How do you communicate with a species that would rather flee from suspicious lion sounds and movements rather than stay around to discover a plastic bag in the bush rather than the lion? How do you reward a species that is not motivated by the tone of your voice, like how you tell your dog…good dog. Good dog! You can pitch your voice just perfect and say, "Good Horse, Good Horse". It means nothing to the horse. Horses are 95% non-verbal animals.

As you progress through your natural horsemanship journey, learning the psychology of communicating with a prey animal is a game changer. The journey causes your humanality to change.

Remember at the start of the book when Dale told me that Jenny was half horse and knew exactly what to do to communicate with the horse? I'm talking about enormous change in yourself as you experience this journey. Your horse changes too. Your horse becomes more human in learning how to think things through rather than the flight response. In turn, you become able to understand non-verbal, prey animal species!

I am a self-proclaimed left brained extrovert, raised as an only child. Only-children like to be the "boss". The Parelli training for humans helped me to become the leader my horses needed. Sage put up a grand left-brained introvert fight for domination, but gradually the knowledge and experience I gained with the Parelli program and Jenny Vaught made me come out the winner.

When I was writing this book, I attended a lecture by Dr. Patrick Handley on Horse and Humanality. At the end of the evening, I and a few other brave souls laid out a humanality chart and the other students secretly annotated which quadrant we fell into.

Some of these students of the horse have known me for years and some for a short time. All of them selected Right Brain Extrovert for me. I was astounded. I thought right brain meant fear and locked up brain, and inability to process situations. That's what I have been taught about right brain horses. Turns out I had made the error of assuming again. Right brain extrovert is a wonderful personality according to the descriptive words on the chart.

I purchased the Horse and Human Match that Dr. Handley and Linda Parelli designed. I wanted to know just who exists in this body! Even better, was the answer. A few answers on the test threw me just barely into the left brain introvert category, but I am so close to being all the four personalities that I've been diagnosed as an "axis" person. "Axie" people can slide all over the chart and be whoever we need to be to communicate or not communicate with others. I attribute my change from self-proclaimed left brain extrovert over to right brain extrovert down to left brain introvert to the changes that I made during this journey with horses. My communication skills, learning how to communicate with others and how to listen to others communicating with me was a 360 kind of personality switch. A natural horsemanship journey with horses changes humans. Riding with Jennifer Vaught as your teacher and inspiration will make you change.

I went through fear one more time that will be coming in the next book. I learned to "name that fear". I ask myself, "Self, what is it that you are actually afraid of?" My "self" stumbles around a bit, sometimes for days as I ponder this question. I have finally figured out, the fear is loss of control. When you lose control of the situation, it becomes an emotional thing. Sometimes, your brain hides the fear from you. Fear can be beaten back. I became a much deeper person from this horsemanship journey and working through fear. I'm so deep now, my nickname is "well"! It is best that you plan ahead for your horse journey and not experience this fear. Fear can take your dream away from you or spoil it.

Velvet and I hit that personality match square on. Our "Susanality" and "Velvetanality" merged into a great bond. The invisible horse gene plays a big part in fighting to win your dream with horses. Other factors determine whether or not you will win through. I hope your horse genes and your choices enable you to win your dream with horses!

The After Words

My pony gene journey has not stopped. I've had more horses and more journey. All horses have their own story with occasional bouts of humorous pathetic tales. There may be more books. Visit my ever continuing blog at http://www.mofoxtrotter.com/viewpoint

References: All the principle people and horses named in this book are still going strong.

Velvet will participate in the 2012 World Celebration in the Versatility Events. Nichole Copple and Velvet won the Youth Versatility garland in the 2012 Spring Show. Both Nichole and Jenny won a blue ribbon on Velvet in the 2012 Spring Show Trail Class. Velvet won many ribbons in 2011 with Jenny Vaught in the Ranch Horse classes. She did become a lesson horse for about two years at Pine Dell Farm. She is a treasure with her shiny black self. Her story continues. Tony told me recently that Velvet has become an exuberant working cow horse and amazed everyone.

Sage has gotten ringbone, but is still a sturdy trail horse. She was a lesson horse for about five years at Pine Dell Farm and many children and adults learned how to ride with Sage. She spent most of those years giving lesson inside an arena. Many people learned about a fox trotter from Sage. I ride her intermittently, as do others. She loves going on trail rides. Her home, along with Velvet, is with me or with Tony and Jenny at For the Horse Ranch.

Tony and Jennifer Vaught are training horses and people in the Kansas City, Springfield, St. Louis and the Florida area. They are adding Texas to their list of clinic locations. http://www.forthehorse.org Email them about training, participating in, or hosting clinics. Visit and study with them at For The Horse Ranch. Occasionally, they need a student apprentice. They are training and showing Missouri Fox Trotters for versatility and ranch horse events. Look for them in the Arabian shows, barrel races and ranch horse versatility with their fox trotters, quarter horses and paints around the Springfield area. They do it all! They do it all with all breeds and all disciplines! Their two daughters, Nichole and Caitlyn, participate in all activities. Justin and baby Aaron help as much as they can with the great adventure called life with horses.

Geno Middleton contines as the Missouri Fox Trotter *winningest* professional performance trainer ever. www.gmstables.net/

Lee Smith is still training people and horses from her ranch in Arizona and all over the USA.
http://www.leesmithdiamonds.com/

Neil Pye heads up Pat Parelli's School of Natural Horsemanship and all the events
Parelli Natural Horsemanship touches the lives of an estimated 200,000 people all over the world.
http://www.parellinaturalhorsetraining.co

The Parelli system of training constantly evolves to bring the best methods of teaching and understand to their human students. You can now get a detailed report of your horse's personality; unique characteristics, motivators, needs, wants, desires, behaviors, etc., along with a report on your own "humanality". This will let you achieve great results by knowing what is uniquely important to that individual horse. This approach to understanding horses helps horses – and us humans – become more balanced, centered and confident.
http://www.parellinaturalhorsetraining.com/horsenality-horses/

David Lichman is a premier Parelli clinician and teacher. David started his horse life in the show ring with Tennessee Walking Horses. He is an expert on gaited horses. "Gaited Horses, Naturally" is a DVD and book training package.
http://www.davidlichman.com

Dave Ellis is a Master Parelli clinician and teacher. He started into the Parelli system with a Tennessee Walking Horse. Dave is an expert on gaited horses. http://www.lsranchnaturally.com/

Ellie Stine-Masek continues teaching dressage.

Nathan Granner is not mentioned in this book. He is my son, an extraordinaire opera singer, extreme wonder miracle. Nathan designed the front cover of this book. He is my eighth wonder on the world! www.nathangranner.com

Deina Wilson www.mofoxtrot.com/wilson continues to be my source of publication encouragement. Deina asked me to write stories to publish on her web site. Without her encouragement to turn my thoughts into stories, we would not have had this book! Deina has switched me over to a blog now. Most of these stories are in the blog. The blog is a much shorter version of these stories. www.mofoxtrot.com/viewpoint.

Dawn Young has been my photographer since I started going to the Missouri Fox Trotter Celebration back in the late 90's. She is www.freereindesign.com. She took the picture on the back of the book of Velvet and I. Thank you Dawn!

I recommend the book, *"Easy Gaited Horses" by Lee Ziegler* to help understand the gaits of most of the gaited horses. The book will help your brain understand. It certainly helps if your body can learn the gaits too. "Feel" is the target word for your body learning.

May Your Horse Genes Have a Happy Life!

"Susan is a great promoter of the Missouri Fox Trotter. Through her humorous journeys, she shows why these fox trotters are the horse of choice for young and old alike. Her many experiences let the readers go along with her and learn many important lessons. This is a must read for all horse lovers, but especially those who love their Missouri Fox Trotters."
Dr. Joyce Graening
Missouri Fox Trotter Horse Breed Association President

"Anybody would want to read this book!"
Dr. Patrick Handley

"I received a funny phone call from a lady I had never met. She said, "Hi, my name is Susan Engle and I have written a book on my trials and tribulations, with my horse!" She then told me I was the reason she had purchased a Missouri Fox Trotter.
Susan proceeded to tell her story of watching me exhibit the best horse I have ever ridden, Missouri's Charming Princess, in the Concert of Champions, at the American Royal, in Kansas City, MO. It was very gratifying when she wanted me to be part of her book. It is a funny, but real life story of the some of the things we have all dealt with regarding life and horses. I wish you the best on your future endeavors with your horse and your book. Thank you for letting me be a part of it!
Thanks so much,"
Geno Middleton